# THE PLANT-BASED DIET FOR BEGINNERS

A COMPLETE GUIDE TO THE PLANT-BASED DIET WITH DELICIOUS RECIPES FOR YOUR WELL-BEING. LET'S KICK-START A HEALTHY EATING AND ENERGIZE YOUR BODY

# TABLE OF CONTENTS

# TABLE OF CONTENTS

# INTRODUCTION

Weight loss is an almost certain result you will enjoy once you start the plant-based diet, but this is not the only benefit that you will enjoy. Think of all those activities you have always wanted to pursue but shelved because you simply had no energy left after your usual day's work.

Well, it's time to dust off those hobbies and the things you enjoy doing, because on the plant-based you will have more energy for your daily work and play! The accompanying mental clarity and sharpness of thought are also positive effects which you will have as a direct result of the diet. A better health report card, by way of optimized cholesterol readings, normalized blood sugar and a corresponding lowered risk of cardiovascular diseases are also just some of the beneficial health effects experienced by most on the diet.

This book's aim is primarily to give you the tools with which to let the diet run more smoothly and seamlessly in your daily life. Something that many learn is that a diet is almost only as good as the number of recipes it has in its repertoire. The benefits of a particular diet may be numerous, but if you are forced to have the same stuff every breakfast, lunch and dinner, even the most avid supporter would probably have problems sustaining the diet. This is where I am most happy to say that the plant-based diet has quite some leeway for the concoction of various different recipes, and it is the purpose of this book to bring you some of the more delicious and easy-to-prepare meals for your gastronomic pleasure!

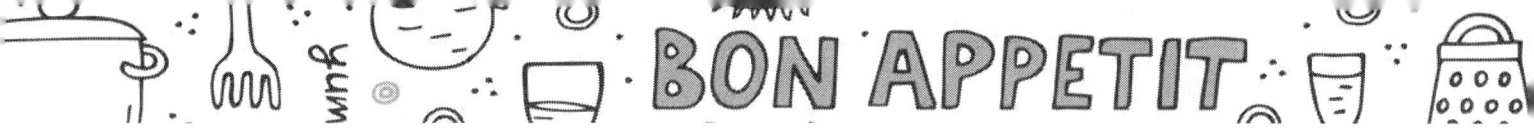

For the beginners as well as the adepts, the recipes contained within are created specifically to be appealing to your palate, while not requiring you to literally spend the whole day in the kitchen! Concise and to the point, the recipes break down meal preparation requirements in a simple step-by-step format, easy for anyone to understand.

Over the past 5 years, scientific articles have shown the substantial benefits of increasing your consumption of plant-based foods. Studies show that adopting a more plant-based diet helps to prevent and even reverse some of the diseases that cause more incidences of death in the Western world, being more successful than medicine or surgery. This type of plant-based diet is the only one shown to reverse the number 1 cause of death by heart attacks. Experts have proven with their studies that by following a low-saturated vegetable diet, rich in complex carbohydrates and basic vegetable-based protein, and changing some lifestyle habits (moving the body at least 30 minutes a day), many illnesses can be reversed.

A vegetable-based diet also helps prevent certain types of cancer, reduces the incidences of heart disease and diabetes, Cholesterolemia, Hypertension, Alzheimer's, Parkinson's Disease, Rheumatoid Arthritis, Ulcers, and Vaginal Infections.

A plant-centered diet has a positive effect on the prevention of accumulation of abdominal fat, the appearance of acne, aging, allergies, asthma, body odor, cellulite, eczema, Metabolic Syndrome, and body weight control.

We can not only increase the chances of improving our life expectancy by increasing our intake of fruits and vegetables, but also ensure a life with a higher quality of health. However, the consumption of meat and other foods of animal origin, including dairy products, have shown that (possibly due to its high content of saturated fats, arachidonic acid, and hemo metal), life expectancy is shortened.

Consumption of meat, fruit, milk, and eggs often increases exposure to toxins, mercury and other heavy metals and xenoestrogens that are produced when fish is cooked at high temperatures, and carcinogenic substances in meat.

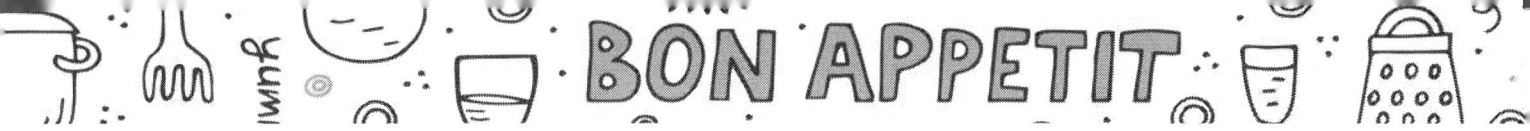

Contrary to popular belief, in their diet, most Vegans do get enough protein, consume more nutrients than the average omnivore, and typically maintain a more appropriate weight. There are only 2 vitamins that we can't find in plant foods; these are vitamin D, that we get from exposure to the sun, and vitamin B12, produced by micro bacteria that live on the earth, and from which one should be supplemented.

# CHAPTER 1:
# HOW A PLANT-BASED DIET CAN IMPROVE YOUR HEALTH

A plant-based diet is essentially a form of diet that helps you to create a diet regime that is completely centred around the consumption of nothing but plant-based produce.

If you think closely, you would easily notice that the core of the diet program is very similar to a vegan diet, where you are not allowed to consume anything other than vegetables. While that is true to a certain extent, certain things might change depending on the variation of the diet that you want to follow.

Since the program is designed to be followed by as many people as possible, the different options allow an individual to choose the one best suited for his/her requirements and lifestyle.

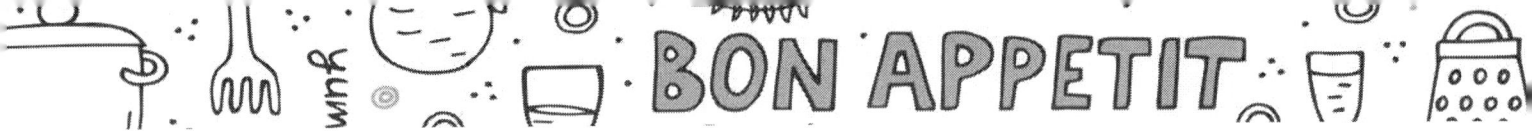

While following the plant-based diet, most people often prefer to follow it in the essence of the purest form of Veganism, while others prefer to have a mix of vegan and vegetarian.

Regardless of which form of the diet you follow, the one main difference between the plant-based diet and all the other vegetable-based diets is that in a plant-based diet, the consumption of any sorts of processed food is strictly prohibited.

That means that you should not go for any sort of packaged/pre-processed food and, instead, opt for healthy and natural alternatives as much as possible.

Now, since I have already mentioned the variations of the program, let me talk a bit more about them next.

The different variations of a plant-based diet

Let's have a look at the different forms of the diet that you should know about.

- *Semi-Vegetarianism*: This program is very loosely based on the core vegetarian program, as it only asks you to be a full vegetarian most of the time while having the option to opt for meat from time to time.

- *Pescatarian*: This is very similar to the Semi-Vegetarian diet program; however, it allows you to have dairy, eggs, shellfish, and fish but no red meat, such as beef, poultry, pork, etc.

- *Macrobiotic Diet*: This variation mostly focuses on the consumption of whole-grain, miso, sea vegetables, vegetables, naturally processed foods, and so on. It is possible to follow through this program without opting for either seafood or other types of animal products.

- *Ovo-Lacto Vegetarianism*: This version of the diet allows you to have dairy and eggs alongside fruits and vegetables.

- *Ovo-Vegetarianism*: This version will allow you to eat eggs alongside fruits and vegetables, but not milk.

- *Fruitarianism*: This version is a form of a vegan diet that mostly surrounds the consumption of fruits. If you have diabetes, then this might be the perfect one for you!

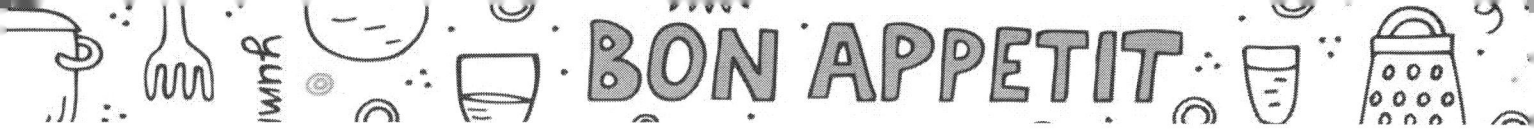

- *Vegetarianism*: Vegetarians mostly prefer to stick to fruits and vegetables, but they also have the liberty to sometimes indulge in eggs and dairy if they choose.

- *Veganism*: This is the most common and well-known form of a plant-based diet and the one that is followed the most around the world. This version will encourage you to consume more legumes, fruits, grains, vegetables, seeds, nuts, etc. while letting go of anything even remotely derived from animals.

Regardless of which variation you choose, always make sure to keep in mind that the main idea is to avoid processed food as much as possible.

## Looking at the Origin of the Diet

Now before moving forward, I would like to share a little bit about the origin of the diet and where it came from. Now, you should keep in mind that the plant-based diet is essentially a modern take on the classic vegetarian and vegan diet, so to understand the roots of the plant-based diet, we must understand the roots of Vegetarianism and Veganism.

While the modern human race is slowly starting to completely embrace the idea of a non-carnivorous diet, as you will soon see, the concept of a plant-based diet has been discussed at various times throughout history.

According to scholars and researchers, the very first group of people who were brave enough to let go of their carnivorous roots and follow a more plant-based path in hopes of achieving a longer life were the Pythagoreans. The Pythagoreans are a group of people who were led, inspired and encouraged by the original teachings of the great Greek philosopher, Pythagoras, during the 6th Century (Before Christ).

After that, evidence was found in the 3rd Century (Anno Domini) scripture titled "Abstinence from Animal Food," where the concepts of a version of a vegan diet were explained. This particular book was written based on the dietary habits of yet another Greek Philosopher named Plotinus.

During the 304 – 232 Before Christ era, evidence solidifying the ideas of vegetarianism were found following the Maurya Dynasty, when the esteemed Ashoka (who was also a Buddhist and vegetarian), inspired his people to take more care of animals and consume plant-

based food as opposed to killing animals for meat.

Following that, the Tang Dynasty emperor Tenmu also took major steps when it came to preventing the hunting and killing of animals by banning the consumption of wild animal meat.

Moving a bit forward now, during the 1400s and the 1700s, respectively, Leonardo Da Vinci and Benjamin Franklin became two of the most iconic and influential figures in history to adopt the vegetarian way of life.

Keeping that in mind, the Vegetarian Diet started coming into the US mass population during the 1800s when John Harvey Kellogg started to encourage people to follow a vegetarian diet that would increase the health and lifespan of the US population.

Kellogg greatly inspired Lenna Frances Cooper, who was a nursing graduate and chief dietician back in 1906. She studied his methods and finally wrote and published a book titled "The New Cookery" in 1913, which was possibly one of the very first cookbooks that solely presented a vast array of vegetable-based diets to experiment with.

Cooper later moved on to co-found the American Dietetic Association in 1917, and after that, the concept of plant-based diet slowly started to reach the mass even more.

She served as the 14th president of the Academy and has been honored with the Lenna Frances Cooper Memorial Lecture Award since 1962.

A note on the impact of a plant-based diet on animal life and environment

Apart from having several different health benefits, a plant-based diet, just like a vegan or vegetarian diet, greatly helps to protect both animal life and the environment.

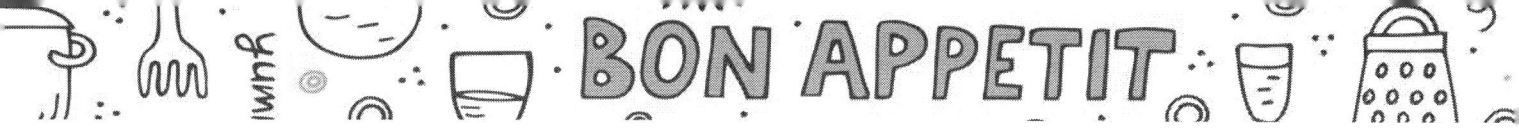

## Regarding Animal Cruelty

When it comes to animal cruelty, it has been predicted by the USDA in 2018 that an average American would eat about 222 pounds of red meat and poultry, excluding eggs, dairy and fish in the days to come.

The majority of animals nowadays are raised for food but are subjected to an extreme level of inhumane practices and are forced to live in tight spaces. The only goal is to feed as many medicines and antibiotics as possible to accelerate their growth. Egg-laying hens are kept in battery cages, female pigs in gestation crates, cows on feedlots, and so on.

They suffer a lot just so that they can provide the growing population within a very short period. The animals who are not up to par, such as sheep with low wool production, dairy cows with low milk production, a hen with low egg supply, are sent directly to the slaughterhouse.

As more and more people are starting to follow the plant-based diet and other similar programs, they are slowly helping to lower the number of such heinous acts and save more animal lives.

## Regarding the Environment

This is another reason why one should follow a plant-based diet. As of 2014, a study published in The American Journal of Clinical Nutrition concluded that plant-based diets are significantly more sustainable when compared to other red meat-based diets.

On the other hand, according to the Food and Agriculture Organization of the United Nations, animal agriculture is leading to the excessive production of greenhouse gasses that are responsible for more than 18% of the world's greenhouse gas emissions.

A very thorough study found in the Journal Climatic Change states that people who completely omitted animal-based products from their diet were responsible for less than half as much greenhouse gas emission as those consuming moderate amounts of animal products.

Not only that, but they need to produce livestock and animals for the ever-growing population is also forcing us to cut down more trees and prepare lands for the animal.

In fact, in 2006, the FAO stated that almost 70% of all agricultural land is used for the culture of livestock.

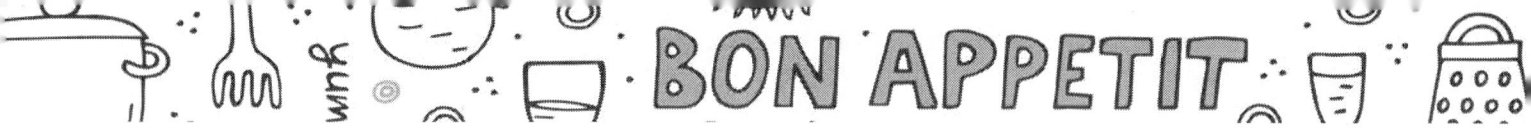

However, a study in 2013, published in the Environmental Research Letters, stated that 36% of calories produced by the world's crops are being used for animal feed and biofuel feedstock, and if everyone made a switch to eating plant-based foods, then we could increase our available food calories by almost 70%, which could then be used to feed an additional 4 billion people.

So, as you can already see, going on a completely plant-based diet won't only save you but will save the world as well!

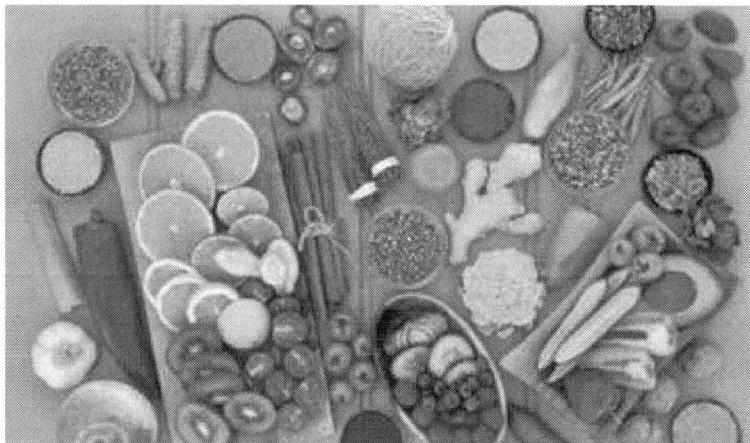

# CHAPTER 2:
# WHAT ARE THE BENEFITS OF A PLANT-BASED DIET

Many people mistake the plant-based diet for a vegan one. So, let's talk about the difference. There are parallels in both of them, but there are small differences. A vegan diet does not include any products based on animals. This, of course, contains meats but also eggs and outcomes of these animals, such as honey. Vegans will carry this perspective into their life as well, which is more than a diet to them. A plant-based diet will keep you from eating anything based on animals, but it will not prevent you from using animal products in your life.

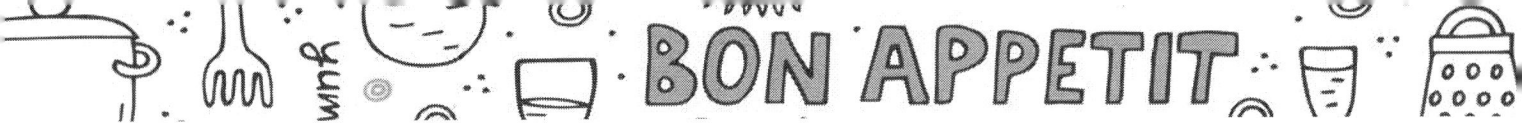

## The Benefits

Now that you know what the plant-based diet is, it's essential to look at the host of benefits that it has to offer. It's hard to stick to a diet that makes you drastically change your current way of eating if you don't have a good reason. That's what this chapter is about. Giving you that good reason to meet your health and weight loss goals using the plant-based diet.

## Lowers Blood Pressure

A plant-based diet has been proven to lower blood pressure because it has a high potassium content. A plant-based diet reduces blood pressure as well as stress and anxiety. Potassium-rich foods include seeds, whole, almonds, beans, berries, and grain. However, meat contains almost no potassium, which is why the plant-based diet offers a better way to control your blood pressure.

## Lowers Cholesterol

Plants don't contain cholesterol, which includes saturated forms such as coffee or chocolate. When you live a plant-based diet lifestyle, you're reducing the amount of cholesterol you take in to next to zero. This plant-based diet will lessen the danger of heart illness and disease since cholesterol is an important cause of stroke and heart attack.

## Maintains Blood Sugar Levels

The plant-based diet has a lot of protein. Protein can lower blood sugar production, and in turn, it will leave you feeling full for longer. Also, a plant-based diet can help to reduce stress levels by lowering the cortisone levels in the body. Cortisol is a stress hormone.

## Staves off Chronic Disease

Chronic diseases, including diabetes, cancer, and obesity, are low in societies that follow a plant-based lifestyle. This diet has been proven to help to fight off chronic disease by helping to reduce chronic inflammation, high blood sugar, stress, and provides your body with the nutrients it needs.

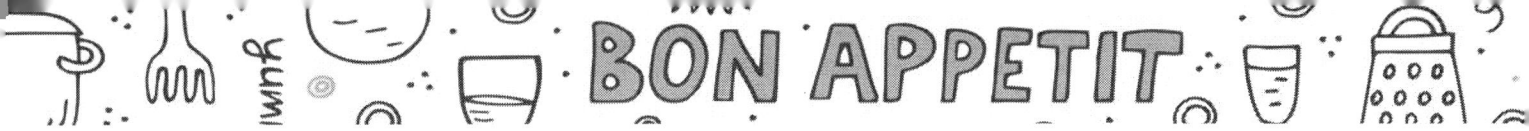

## Weight Loss

In societies that follow a mainly plant-based lifestyle, obesity is also lower, which we've already covered as a chronic disease. Since you're taking in more vitamins and nutrients as well as fiber, which your body has to break down. While you're eating a plant-based lifestyle, you're also likely to stay fuller for longer, which means you'll eat less overall. To lose weight, you have to burn more calories than you take in, so eating less is an essential part of that.

## More Energy

Within days of this type of eating, you'll feel energized because you'll get the nutrients you need. The foods that you'll be eating will also have higher water content, which can hydrate your skin and leave you feeling better overall. Plant-based foods are easier to digest and lighter, so you'll feel better than ever in just a few days. You'll also get a better sleep when you eat right. When you feed your body the vitamins and minerals it needs, you'll help your body relax and give it a peaceful sleep. Calcium and magnesium can help to relax the body for quiet rest, which this diet is packed full of.

# CHAPTER 3:
# WHOLE-FOODS

The first step to following a whole food plant-based diet is understanding what it means. To put it plain and simple, it means filling a majority of your diet with foods that are not processed or refined and come directly from plants. They are foods that are as close as possible to their original source and are completely unmodified. It is not a diet restricted solely to fruits and vegetables; there are many delicious alternatives to help you have a satisfying choice of foods to eat.

## Get your Phytochemicals

The only place to get phytochemicals is in whole foods, such as fruits, vegetables, beans and whole grains. These essential nutrients have a direct impact on your health. The latest research determines that a few of the key phytochemicals might help to prevent certain cancers, lower cholesterol, keep the gastrointestinal tract healthy and protect

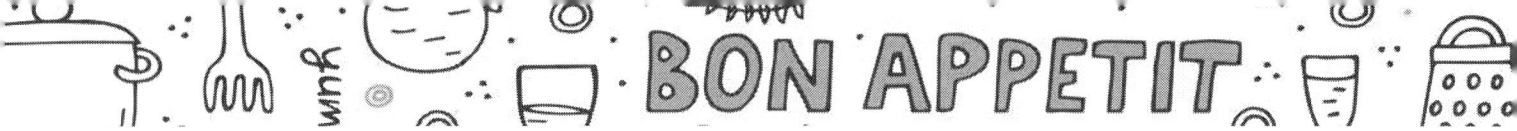

various cells throughout the body. There are thousands of different forms available, but the most commonly known nutrients are terms that might be a little more familiar to you: flavonoids, antioxidants and carotenoids.

How do you fill your diet with these amazing nutrients? Start by creating a rainbow of colors on your plates. The more colorful fruits and vegetables that you consume, the higher the chances of consuming the nutrients your body needs. There are many beautiful colored fruits and vegetables to choose from including red tomatoes, blue blueberries, orange carrots, pink watermelon, pink grapefruit, green spinach, green kale, red strawberries and red raspberries. The more colors on your plate, the more benefits you are providing your body.

In addition to fruits and vegetables, phytonutrients can be found in whole grain bread, whole grain cereal, walnuts, sunflower seeds, peas, lentils, green tea and black tea. If you do consume breads and cereals, it is important to ensure that they are truly made from whole grains, not processed grains which could be stripped of the nutrients you assume you are obtaining by eating it.

## Is Organic a Requirement?

Eating whole foods does not mean that they must be locally grown or even organic; that is a completely different topic. This does not mean that your whole foods cannot be organic; it is just not a prerequisite to qualify as whole or natural. Obviously, organic or locally grown food could provide you with the added benefit of eliminating harmful toxins and chemicals, which can further the health benefit of eating whole foods.

## Maximize Nutrients in Vegetables

The reason that we eat food, besides that it tastes good, is to obtain the vital nutrients necessary for good health. When you consume food that has been modified, processed or refined, the important nutrients are removed. This is even true for those foods that you consider healthy. For example, you might think you are doing your body good by eating spinach or broccoli. But if you do not eat it raw or prepare it properly, you are likely losing some of its nutrients, especially those that are water soluble. Vitamin B and C are two of the water-soluble vitamins found in both vegetables that are lost when these vegetables are cooked in water, whether boiled or steamed.

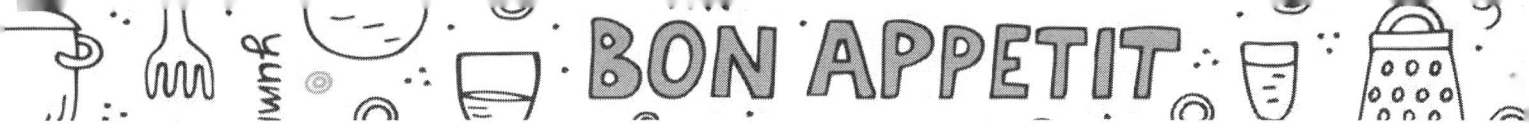

Choosing to eat these vegetables raw is the best way to consume all vital nutrients. If you prefer them cooked, choose methods such as sautéing, stir frying or blanching as each of these methods are considered "quick cooking" methods and avoid the risk of losing many nutrients.

## Choosing Whole Grains

In addition to eating fruits and vegetables, a whole foods diet also includes eating a variety of whole grains. Care should be taken when you choose your grains, however. Not all whole grains are as "whole" as they sound. When you choose the right grains, you can reap the benefits of complex carbohydrates as well as vital vitamins and nutrients, adding taste, texture and proper nutrition to your diet.

Grains are found in the seeds of various grasses. They can be found in various forms including wheat, oats, rice, cornmeal and barley. When grains start out, they are considered whole and their most important ingredients bran and germ are intact. It is during the processing of these grains that they are stripped of bran and germ as well as their vital nutrients. This is what results in refined and enriched grains, which make up the products that have a longer shelf life, such as white bread and white rice. These foods, as you probably know, are less healthy for you. When you read product labels, look for the words refined or enriched grains and steer clear. In refined grains, the lost nutrients are never replaced. In enriched grains, the products are fortified with the stripped nutrients, but it does not provide the same benefits as eating whole foods with the natural nutrients right from the start.

## Creating the Perfect Meals

Creating the perfect meals with the right plant based whole foods does not have to be difficult. In fact, it is best to get creative in order to maximize the nutrients that you consume. Start with the basics including whole grain breads, whole grain pasta, steel cut oats, colorful fruits and raw vegetables. Then you can get creative:

- Add fruits and spices to your oatmeal

- Add flax seed to your whole grain cereal

- Make salad the main course for lunch or dinner and get creative

- Add your favorite vegetables to whole grain pasta or rice

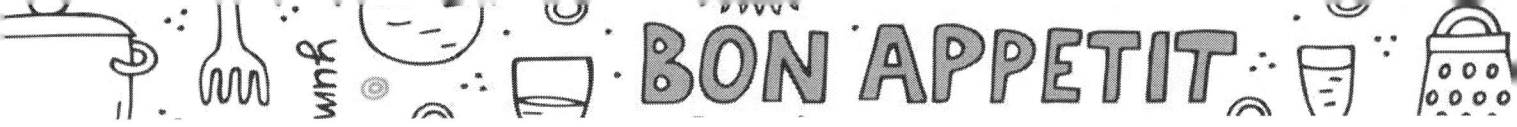

- Make smoothies with as many fruits and vegetables as possible

- Add plant based, natural nut butters to whole grain bread

- Eat fruit for dessert

- Add beans to lunch and dinner entrées

- Include at least one fruit and vegetable at every meal

# CHAPTER: 4:
# TIPS FOR THIS DIET

Here are some tips to get you started so you can stick to this diet with ease!

## Look for Milk Alternatives

There are many non-dairy milk alternatives out there. There is coconut, cashew, Brazil nut, rice, almond and even hemp seed milk substitutes out there. Most can be used in equal measurements, especially in baking. Just make sure you're using their unsweetened versions. The best is that most of these kinds of milk are rich in calcium so you won't be missing out.

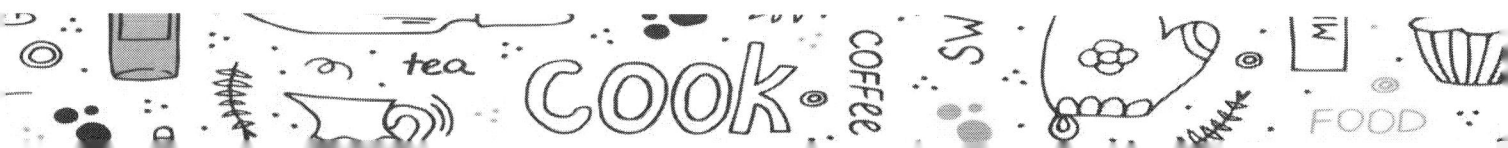

Rice Milk · Hemp Milk · Cow Milk · Soy Milk · Almond Milk · Goat Milk

## Look for Egg Alternatives

You can also replace eggs in recipes. You can use six tablespoons of water with three tablespoons of chia seeds or ground flaxseeds. Just soak them for five to ten minutes so that the mixture becomes gelatinous. You can also use a quarter cup of pureed banana or a quarter cup of applesauce. Depending on the recipe. Each one of these is the equivalent of a single egg.

1/4 Cup Applesauce

1/2 Mashed Banana

Commercial Egg Replacer

1 Tbsp Vinegar + tsp Baking Soda

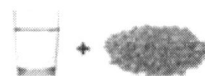

INSTEAD OF AN EGG

1 Tbsp Ground Flax Seed+ 3 tbsp Water

1/4 Cup Silken Tofu

1/4 Cup Soy Yogurt

## Look for Cheese Alternatives

*There isn't a substitute for cheese, but the plant world does have soft and creamy textures that can take the place of cheese. It does make a small change in the taste of the dish, but it isn't too bad. The most popular replacements are soaked and blended cashews, sliced avocado, sprouted soft organic tofu, and nutritional yeast.*

## Look for Meat Alternatives

For a rich, hearty texture that will help to fill you up, there are beans, Portobello mushrooms, tempeh, and tofu. Each of these is chewy and hearty, and they can be marinated to get different flavours. You can also use these for chili, stews, and burgers or can be served baked.

## Be Careful Eating Out

It can be hard to dine out when you're trying to enjoy a plant-based diet. However, there are many restaurants that offer vegan options, so try to look for one in advance. Just realize that you'll need to minimize the number of times you eat out. However, if you need to go out, then check out the menu online before you arrive. Look for dishes that are low in fat and full of vegetables, and then look for grilled, baked and steamed options. Try to avoid any dishes that are fried, rich, creamy or crispy. Just don't be shy about asking for a different salad dressing or side dish either. Make sure sauces and cheeses are left out too. If there's bread, ask for whole wheat. If there is rice, ask for brown rice.

## Purge Your Kitchen

It's best that you get rid of any temptation that's in your kitchen and calling your name if you're trying to start a plant-based diet. It's not good to have unhealthy foods in front of you, or you're bound to give in.

## Plan Your Meals

Luckily this book comes with a meal plan that will help you to stick to your first three weeks of your diet. However, you may want to stick to planning your meals for the first few months if you find yourself struggling.

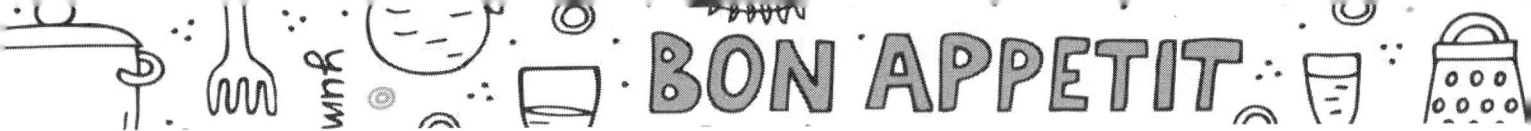

### Choose the One for You

You can choose the plant-based diet for you! Here are some of the most common plant-based diets out there.

- **Veganism:** This is a diet that includes legumes, fruits, grains, vegetables, nuts and seeds, but you'll not be able to eat any food that's sourced from animals.

- **Raw Veganism:** This is a diet that includes uncooked and some dehydrated foods.

- **Vegetarianism:** This is a diet that consists of legumes, vegetables, nuts and fruit. You can include eggs and dairy in this diet, but you aren't allowed meat.

- **Fruitarianism:** This is a vegan diet that primarily involves fruit, but you should not use this if you are diabetic.

- **Ovo-Lacto Vegetarianism:** This encourages that you eat eggs and dairy along with your fruit and vegetables.

- **Ovo Vegetarianism:** This is where you are allowed to eat eggs with your fruits and vegetables, but you still can't have dairy.

- **Lacto Vegetarianism:** This allows you to have dairy but no eggs with your fruits and vegetables.

- **Semi-Vegetarianism:** This is a mostly vegetarian diet with the occasional time that you can have meat.

- **Pescatarian:** This is a semi-vegetarian diet that allows you to have dairy, eggs, shellfish and fish.

- **Macrobiotic Diet:** This diet highlights whole grains, beans, miso soup, sea vegetables, vegetables, and naturally processed foods. This can be done with or without seafood and other animal products.

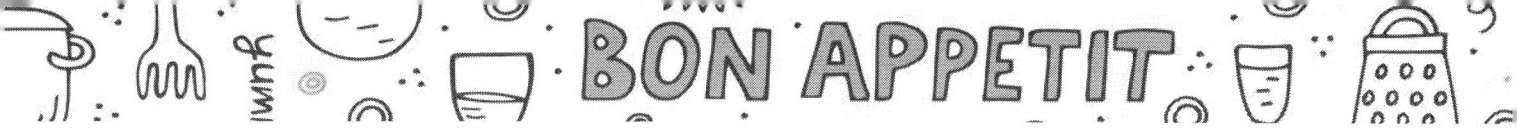

# CHAPTER 5:
# WHAT TO AVOID AND WHAT TO EAT

Now let's get down to the real business at hand. What do we get to eat, and what are we eliminating? It is best to have this decided, but you can always make changes as you become more accustomed. Everybody has different tastes and dislikes, so the more thought you put into this area, the clearer your guidelines will be.

In order to get the best out of your plant-based diet, you will want to set a path and boundaries for yourself. This will help to ensure your success, and help you to maximize your results. The best way to go about this is to make it as fun and enjoyable for you as possible! Make yourself templates and sample lists and menus that will inspire you, and help you decide what will work best for you. Start out with a pen

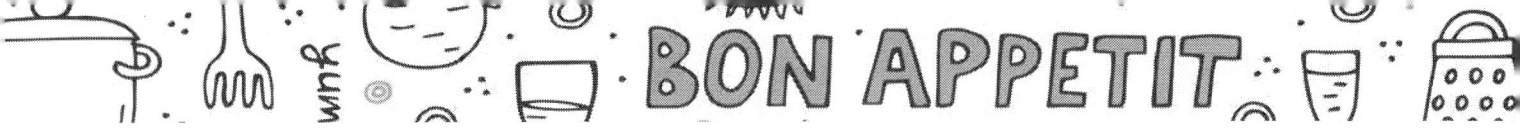

or pencil, and paper. Write down what you currently eat. Try to get the clearest idea of what you eat day in and day out. You may want to keep a food journal for about a week, but for some this won't be a pleasurable experience. But what you can do is think of all of the foods that you normally eat, be entirely honest, and place them each in one of two categories: Do Eat, and Do Not Eat.

The foods you will continue to eat, you will place under Do Eat. The foods you will plan to avoid, at least temporarily, you will place under Do Not Eat. Seems simple enough, right? Now, you should do this slowly, and over time. Choose only a few foods to adopt, and to eliminate from your diet at a time. This will be a gradual transition. You may even want to make a third category marked Why? This category is a great place to note why you are choosing to add or eliminate that food, in case you need a reminder.

Foods to Eat

*Vegetables*

- **Kale**
- **Broccoli**
- **Cucumber**
- **Celery**
- **Ginger**
- **Sweet Potato**
- **Bell Peppers**
- **Carrots**
- **Corn**
- **Cucumbers**
- **Garlic**
- **Ginger**
- **Mushrooms**
- **Onions**
- **Potatoes**

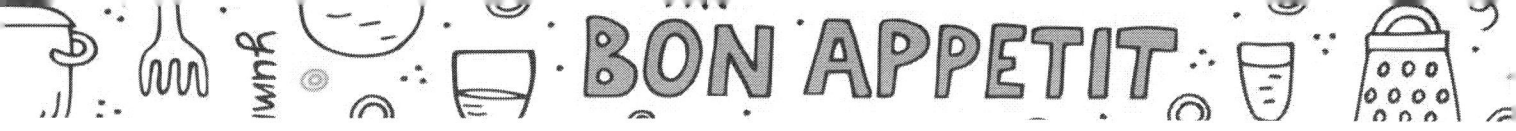

- Tomatoes (technically fruit)
- Avocado (also a fruit)
- Zucchini

*Fruits*

- Banana
- Apple
- Orange
- Grapefruit
- Grapes
- Pineapple
- Berries
- Lemons and Limes
- Pears

*Grains*

- Brown Rice
- Sprouted or Gluten Free Bread
- Rice or gluten free Noodles
- Quinoa
- Steel Cut Oats
- Tortillas or Taco shells

*Proteins*

- Tofu
- Tempeh
- Beans
- Lintels
- Nuts
- Nut Butters

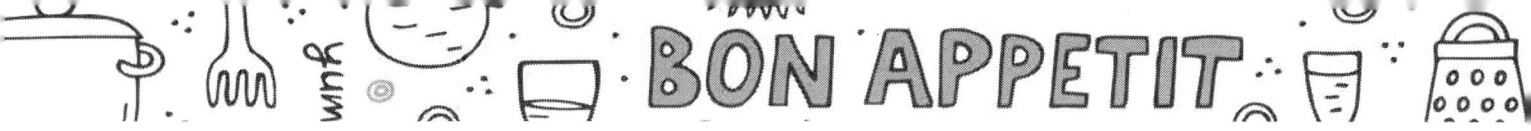

- **Seeds**
- **Chia Seeds**
- **Chickpeas**
- **Edamame**
- **Flax Seed**
- **Hummus**
- **Quinoa**
- **Tahini**
- **Dark Leafy Green Vegetables**

*Frozen Foods*

- **Dairy-free ice cream/ sorbets**
- **Frozen Veggies**
- **Frozen Fruit**

*Condiments*

- **Hot Sauce**
- **Ketchup**
- **Tahini**
- **Soy Sauce**

*Other Foods*

- **Canned Goods**
- **Beans**
- **Coconut Milk**
- **Tomatoes**
- **Tomato Paste**
- **Pantry Essentials**
- **Bouillon Cubes**
- **Dried Fruit**

- **Nutritional Yeast**
- **Oils**
- **Olives**
- **Marinara Sauce**
- **Vinegars**
- **Agave Syrup**
- **Vanilla Extract**
- **Baking Soda**
- **Baking Powder**
- **Chocolate, dark or dairy free**
- **Cocoa powder, unsweetened**
- **Sugar**
- **Flour**
- **Maple Syrup**

*Spices*

- **Basil**
- **Black Pepper**
- **Chili Powder**
- **Ground Cinnamon**
- **Ground Cumin**
- **Curry Powder**
- **Garam Masala**
- **Garlic Powder**
- **Onion Powder**
- **Oregano**
- **Paprika**

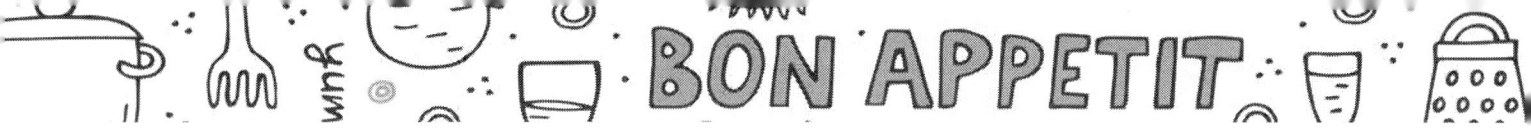

- **Rosemary**
- **Salt (iodized)**
- **Ground Turmeric**
- **Thyme**

## Foods to Eliminate

Adding the right life-supporting foods to your life will go a long way toward helping you achieve the health you desire. It will give you the nutrients and enzymes to make your body work harmoniously. However, adding helpful foods is only part of the food equation. Your body is constantly working to build healthy cells, and to discard of the dead unhealthy material. This process of detoxification is an essential body function. It protects us against destructive toxins and damaged cells. Left unchecked without being removed these toxins can wreak havoc on your, and has the potential to destroy perfectly healthy cells and organs. The detoxification process is just as important as eating nutrient rich foods. The absolute best way to remove unhealthy foods and harmful toxins from your body is to avoid eating them in the first place.

I have composed a basic list of foods and ingredients that should be removed from your kitchen, and your everyday diet. Eliminating these foods will help you achieve the cleanest possible dietary health.

## Reduce or Eliminate:

- **All animal products**
- **Honey (if going full vegan, or eliminating for any reason)**
- **Dairy products**
- **High fructose corn syrup (All refined sugars)**
- **Partially hydrogenated oils**
- **Enriched/ bleached flours**
- **Foods with a very long list of unnatural ingredients**
- **Monosodium glutamate**
- **Foods enriched or fortified with unnatural vitamins**

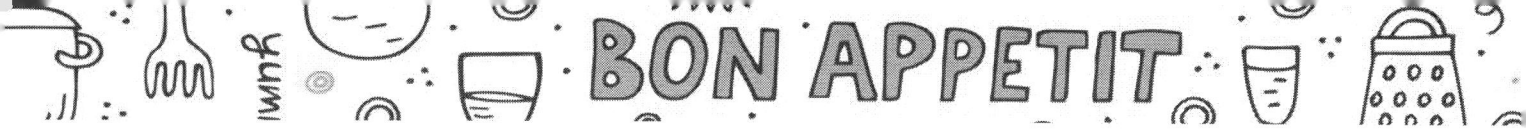

\*This happens when the food has been extracted, and separated from its natural state. It is then usually added with essential trace elements and vitamins. This is not the way we want to consume our food.

Side note: Usually the fact that foods that have long scientific sounding ingredients means that they were made in a lab. This doesn't fair well once in the body.

## Learning to Read Labels

Adopting a new eating style and becoming more aware of what is coming into your body can be a pretty overwhelming endeavor. But with the right knowledge and a lot of practice, you will be able to find out what is in anything you are eating, and you will be able to decide for yourself if it is something that you will choose to eat. The first step to improving something is awareness. Once you have a better idea of what goes into your food, you can move away from the unnatural foods and closer to natural, wholesome nutrition.

For many people, the nutritional facts on a food means very little, when it comes to making food choices. For one, it can be a challenge to understand exactly how nutritional information correlates to what is going on in your body. I think that the number or calories is probably at the most basic level understanding how to use food labels. Basically, you need a certain number of calories per day, to maintain your body weight and current level of nutrition. Your body uses a certain range of calories daily, just by being alive and moving around. The more physical activity you get, the more calories are burned. The more calorie-filled foods you eat, the more calories are stored in your body, usually as fat. Having more muscle on your body means that you can burn more fat.

There are, of course, many other factors that come into play when your body metabolizes food.

## Macros & Vitamins

Another basic gauge for judging your food's nutritional value is the division or macros. What is your meal primarily composed of? This is referring to the type of food, and how it will generally be used in the body. Fat, protein and carbohydrates make up your macros. Also important are the amount of sugar and the amount of salt.

### Fat

Fat is either used immediately in the presence of physical activity, or it will be stored as fat in the body. Fat is stored up in case we are ever faced with a food shortage and need to be protected against starvation. In most developed countries, unless you have a specific life complication where you go hungry often, we do not have a food shortage. We have a surplus of calorie-dense food that is devoid of any nutrition. This is where much of our excess fat comes from.

But all fats are not created equal. Our bodies actually really need fat to be healthy, lustrous, and to feel satisfied by our meals. You want to get plenty of good fats in your diet to keep the right balance. Healthy fats are unrefined, and come mostly from plants, nuts and seeds. Truth be told, healthy fats can also be found in certain types of fish and seafood. Things like avocados and coconut oil provide wonderful healthy fats. So, do nuts and seeds like flax and chia. Snack on plenty of nuts and seeds!

### Protein:

This nutrient is the main ingredient to building our cells and muscles. Protein is what gives us our lean, powerful muscles. Protein helps us to metabolize fat, and helps to regulate your blood sugar. It also benefits your physical performance abilities, not to mention it also really helps to fill you up without having to eat a lot of extra calories. With the right combination, you can make protein work for you to create the body and the health you strive for.

### Carbohydrates

This is essentially your sugar, for your physical energy. Your carbohydrates are either filled with a good source of fiber, or turned into sugar- to be used immediately, or stored as fat.

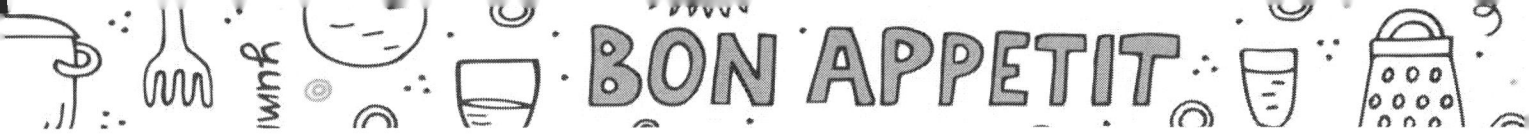

When it comes to the ingredients list, the first 5 ingredients make up most of that food, and contain about 95% of the whole. All ingredients descend in order of concentration. Look out for chemical-laden ingredients which are hard to pronounce, and sound unfamiliar or not descriptive of what it is originally derived from. Look for whole ingredients that are un-tampered with. And if you choose to eat something you know has unhealthy ingredients, then make sure you enjoy it, count it as a treat (or cheat meal), and make up for it moving forward at the next meal.

I also want you to be aware of the order in which your food is digested. Different foods have different schedules of when they enter and exit the body. They also require different enzymes and ph balances to be properly digested. Now, if you have quite a strong gut, you may not need this step. But if you are experiencing noticeable digestive issues, then food combining may make a big difference for you.

*Here is a general guideline for combining your foods effectively and each food approximate digestion time:*

- Eat melon alone (takes 15-30 minutes)

- Eat fruits alone (1-2 hours)

- Starches like grains, roots, beans, and bread items can be eaten with vegetables (3 hours)

- Proteins like nuts, seeds beans and meat go great with vegetables (4 hours, but animal protein can take 8 hours or longer)

- Avoid mixing protein and starched. They do not work well together.

- Avoid mixing fruit and protein- or starch and fruit. This can create rotting in the gut.

- Enjoy avocados with just about anything!

- Veggies are compatible with anything!

# CHAPTER 6:
# 21-DAY MEAL PLAN

| DAY | BREAKFAST | LUNCH | SNACKS | DINNER | DESSERT |
|---|---|---|---|---|---|
| 1 | MAX POWER SMOOTHIE | LIME-MINT SOUP | CINNAMON BAKED APPLE CHIPS | STEAMED CAULIFLOWER | AVOCADO HUMMUS |
| 2 | CHAI CHIA SMOOTHIE | SAVORY SPLIT PEA SOUP | ACORN SQUASH WITH MANGO CHUTNEY | CAJUN SWEET POTATOES | PLANT BASED CRISPY FALAFEL |
| 3 | TROPI-KALE BREEZE | KALE AND LENTIL STEW | HEALTHY CARROT CHIPS | SMOKY COLESLAW | WAFFLES WITH ALMOND FLOUR |
| 4 | HYDRATION STATION | FOUR-CAN CHILI | HEARTY BRUSSELS AND PISTACHIO | MEDITERRANEAN HUMMUS PIZZA | SIMPLE BANANA FRITTERS |
| 5 | MANGO MADNESS | SAUTÉED COLLARD GREENS | BUFFALO CASHEWS | BAKED BRUSSELS SPROUTS | COCONUT AND BLUEBERRIES ICE CREAM |
| 6 | CHOCOLATE PB SMOOTHIE | CREAM OF MUSHROOM SOUP | MORNING PEACH | MINTED PEAS | PEACH CROCKPOT PUDDING |
| 7 | PINK PANTHER SMOOTHIE | CAULIFLOWER AND HORSERADISH SOUP | STICKY MANGO RICE | BASIC BAKED POTATOES | RASPBERRIES & CREAM ICE CREAM |
| 8 | BANANA NUT SMOOTHIE | CURRY LENTIL SOUP | PECAN AND BLUEBERRY CRUMBLE | GLAZED CURRIED CARROTS | HEALTHY CHOCOLATE MOUSSE |
| 9 | OVERNIGHT OATS ON THE GO | CHICKPEA NOODLE SOUP | HEALTHY RICE PUDDING | MISO SPAGHETTI SQUASH | FRUITS, PINE NUTS AND MINT SALAD |
| 10 | OATMEAL BREAKFAST COOKIES | MEXICAN LENTIL SOUP | APPLE SLICES | GARLIC AND HERB NOODLES | VEGAN MINI GINGERBREAD LOAVES |

| DAY | BREAKFAST | LUNCH | SNACKS | DINNER | DESSERT |
|-----|-----------|-------|--------|--------|---------|
| 11 | SUNSHINE MUFFINS | PORTOBELLO MUSHROOM STEW | OATMEAL COOKIES | THAI ROASTED BROCCOLI | VEGAN CHOCOLATE TURRON |
| 12 | APPLESAUCE CRUMBLE MUFFINS | ROOT VEGETABLE STEW | EASY PORTOBELLO MUSHROOMS | COCONUT CURRY NOODLE | VEGAN CHOCOLATE ORANGE TRUFFLES |
| 13 | BAKED BANANA FRENCH TOAST WITH RASPBERRY SYRUP | BLACK BEAN AND QUINOA STEW | THE GARBANZO BEAN EXTRAVAGANZA | COLLARD GREEN PASTA | GLUTEN-FREE CHOCOLATE ORANGE VEGAN CAKE |
| 14 | CINNAMON APPLE TOAST | VEGETARIAN GUMBO | ROASTED ONIONS AND GREEN BEANS | JALAPENO RICE NOODLES | COCONUT SNOWBALLS |
| 15 | MUESLI AND BERRIES BOWL | BRUSSELS SPROUTS STEW | LEMONY SPROUTS | RAINBOW SOBA NOODLES | CHAMPAGNE JELLY WITH FRUITS AND BERRIES |
| 16 | WHOLE-WHEAT BLUEBERRY MUFFINS | SPINACH SOUP WITH DILL AND BASIL | SAUSAGE ROLLS | SPICY PAD THAI PASTA | ORANGES WITH CINNAMON AND HONEY |
| 17 | WALNUT CRUNCH BANANA BREAD | COCONUT WATERCRESS SOUP | ONION RINGS | LINGUINE WITH WINE SAUCE | GREEN BUCKWHEAT COFFEE CAKE |
| 18 | PLANT-POWERED PANCAKES | ROASTED RED PEPPER AND BUTTERNUT SQUASH SOUP | ALMOND-DATE ENERGY BITES | CHEESY MACARONI WITH BROCCOLI | SWEET CHOCOLATE HUMMUS |
| 19 | MAPLE-PECAN GRANOLA | TOMATO PUMPKIN SOUP | PUMPKIN PIE CUPS (PRESSURE COOKER) | SOBA NOODLES WITH TOFU | FRUITS AND BERRIES IN ORANGE JUICE SALAD |
| 20 | PARADISE ISLAND OVERNIGHT OATMEAL | CAULIFLOWER SPINACH SOUP | FUDGY BROWNIES (PRESSURE COOKER) | PLANT BASED KETO LO MEIN | TROPICAL FRUITS SALAD |

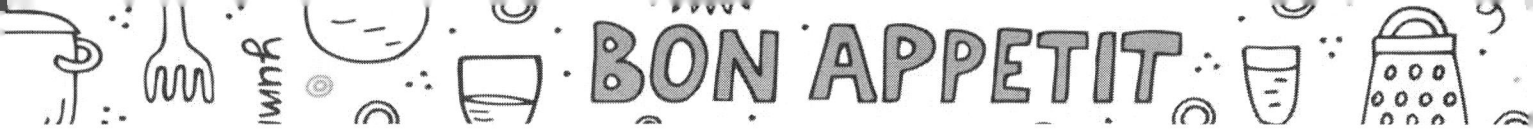

| DAY | BREAKFAST | LUNCH | SNACKS | DINNER | DESSERT |
|---|---|---|---|---|---|
| 21 | PUMPKIN PIE OATMEAL | AVOCADO MINT SOUP | CHOCOLATE PUDDING | VEGETARIAN CHOW MEIN | PEANUT PASTE (HALVA) |

**The following recipes are all present in the next chapters!**

**Also, you can create your own customized 21 Day Meal Plan using the other recipes presented in the next chapters.**

**Stay healthy and Enjoy!**

# CHAPTER 7:
# SMOOTHIES AND BREAKFASTS RECIPES

# 1. MAX POWER SMOOTHIE

## INGREDIENTS

- 1 banana
- ¼ cup rolled oats, or 1 scoop plant protein powder
- 1 tablespoon flaxseed, or chia seeds
- 1 cup raspberries, or other berries
- 1 cup chopped mango (frozen or fresh)
- ½ cup non-dairy milk (optional)
- 1 cup water

## DIRECTIONS

1. Purée everything in a blender until smooth, adding more water (or non-dairy milk) if needed.
2. Add none, some, or all of the bonus boosters, as desired. Purée until blended.

**Nutritions:** *Calories: 550, Total fat: 9g, Carbs: 116g, Fiber: 29g, Protein: 13g*

# 2. CHAI CHIA SMOOTHIE

## INGREDIENTS

- 1 banana
- ½ cup coconut milk
- 1 cup water
- 1 cup alfalfa sprouts (optional)
- 1 to 2 soft Medjool dates, pitted
- 1 tablespoon chia seeds, or ground flax or hemp hearts
- ¼ teaspoon ground cinnamon
- Pinch ground cardamom
- 1 tablespoon grated fresh ginger, or ¼ teaspoon ground ginger

## DIRECTIONS

1. Purée everything in a blender until smooth, adding more water (or coconut milk) if needed.

**Nutritions:** *Calories: 477, Total fat: 29g, Carbs: 57g, Fiber: 14g, Protein: 8g*

# 3. TROPI-KALE BREEZE

## INGREDIENTS

- 1 cup chopped pineapple (frozen or fresh)
- 1 cup chopped mango (frozen or fresh)
- ½ to 1 cup chopped kale
- ½ avocado
- ½ cup coconut milk
- 1 cup water, or coconut water
- 1 teaspoon matcha green tea powder (optional)

## DIRECTIONS

1. Purée everything in a blender until smooth, adding more water (or coconut milk) if needed.

**Nutritions:** *Calories: 566, Total fat: 36g, Carbs: 66g, Fiber: 12g, Protein: 8g*

# 4. HYDRATION STATION

## INGREDIENTS

- 1 banana
- 1 orange, peeled and sectioned, or 1 cup pure orange juice
- 1 cup strawberries (frozen or fresh)
- 1 cup chopped cucumber
- ½ cup coconut water
- 1 cup water
- ½ cup ice

## DIRECTIONS

1. Purée everything in a blender until smooth, adding more water if needed.
2. Add bonus boosters, as desired. Purée until blended.

**Nutritions:** *Calories: 320, Total fat: 3g, Carbs: 76g, Fiber: 13g, Protein: 6g*

# 5. MANGO MADNESS

## INGREDIENTS

- 1 banana
- 1 cup chopped mango (frozen or fresh)
- 1 cup chopped peach (frozen or fresh)
- 1 cup strawberries
- 1 carrot, peeled and chopped (optional)
- 1 cup water

## DIRECTIONS

1. Purée everything in a blender until smooth, adding more water if needed.

**Nutritions:** *Calories: 376, Total fat: 2g, Carbs: 95g, Fiber: 14g, Protein: 5g*

# 6. CHOCOLATE PB SMOOTHIE

## INGREDIENTS

- 1 banana
- ¼ cup rolled oats, or 1 scoop plant protein powder
- 1 tablespoon flaxseed, or chia seeds
- 1 tablespoon unsweetened cocoa powder
- 1 tablespoon peanut butter, or almond or sunflower seed butter
- 1 tablespoon maple syrup (optional)
- 1 cup alfalfa sprouts, or spinach, chopped (optional)
- ½ cup non-dairy milk (optional)
- 1 cup water

## DIRECTIONS

1. Purée everything in a blender until smooth, adding more water (or non-dairy milk) if needed.
2. Add bonus boosters, as desired. Purée until blended.

**Nutritions:** *Calories: 474, Total fat: 16g, Carbs: 79g, Fiber: 18g, Protein: 13g*

# 7. PINK PANTHER SMOOTHIE

## INGREDIENTS

- 1 cup strawberries
- 1 cup chopped melon (any kind)
- 1 cup cranberries, or raspberries
- 1 tablespoon chia seeds
- ½ cup coconut milk, or other non-dairy milk
- 1 cup water

## DIRECTIONS

1. Purée everything in a blender until smooth, adding more water (or coconut milk) if needed.
2. Add bonus boosters, as desired. Purée until blended.

**Nutritions:** *Calories: 459, Total fat: 30g, Carbs: 52g, Fiber: 19g, Protein: 8g*

# 8. BANANA NUT SMOOTHIE

## INGREDIENTS

- 1 banana
- 1 tablespoon almond butter, or sunflower seed butter
- ¼ teaspoon ground cinnamon
- Pinch ground nutmeg
- 1 to 2 tablespoons dates, or maple syrup
- 1 tablespoon ground flaxseed, or chia, or hemp hearts
- ½ cup non-dairy milk (optional)
- 1 cup water

## DIRECTIONS

1. Purée everything in a blender until smooth, adding more water (or non-dairy milk) if needed.

**Nutritions:** *Calories: 343, Total fat: 14g, Carbs: 55g, Fiber: 8g, Protein: 6g*

# 9. OVERNIGHT OATS ON THE GO

## INGREDIENTS

**BASIC OVERNIGHT OATS**
- ½ cup rolled oats, or quinoa flakes for gluten-free
- 1 tablespoon ground flaxseed, or chia seeds, or hemp hearts
- 1 tablespoon maple syrup, or coconut sugar (optional)
- ¼ teaspoon ground cinnamon (optional)

**TOPPING OPTIONS**
- 1 apple, chopped, and 1 tablespoon walnuts
- 2 tablespoons dried cranberries and 1 tablespoon pumpkin seeds
- 1 pear, chopped, and 1 tablespoon cashews
- 1 cup sliced grapes and 1 tablespoon sunflower seeds
- 1 banana, sliced, and 1 tablespoon peanut butter
- 2 tablespoons raisins and 1 tablespoon hazelnuts
- 1 cup berries and 1 tablespoon unsweetened coconut flakes

## DIRECTIONS

1. Mix the oats, flax, maple syrup, and cinnamon (if using) together in a bowl or to-go container (a travel mug or short thermos works beautifully).
2. Pour enough cool water over the oats to submerge them, and stir to combine. Leave to soak for a minimum of half an hour, or overnight.
3. Add your choice of toppings.

**Nutritions:** *Calories: 244, Total fat: 6g, Carbs: 30g, Fiber: 6g, Protein: 7g*

# 10. OATMEAL BREAKFAST COOKIES

## INGREDIENTS

- 1 tablespoon ground flaxseed
- 2 tablespoons almond butter, or sunflower seed butter
- 2 tablespoons maple syrup
- 1 banana, mashed
- 1 teaspoon ground cinnamon
- ¼ teaspoon ground nutmeg (optional)
- Pinch sea salt
- ½ cup rolled oats
- ¼ cup raisins, or dark chocolate chips

## DIRECTIONS

1. Preheat the oven to 350°F. Line a large baking sheet with parchment paper.
2. Mix the ground flax with just enough water to cover it in a small dish, and leave it to sit.
3. In a large bowl, mix together the almond butter and maple syrup until creamy, then add the banana. Add the flax-water mixture.
4. Sift the cinnamon, nutmeg, and salt into a separate medium bowl, then stir into the wet mixture.
5. Add the oats and raisins, and fold in.
6. From 3 to 4 tablespoons batter into a ball and press lightly to flatten onto the baking sheet. Repeat, spacing the cookies 2 to 3 inches apart.
7. Bake for 12 minutes, or until golden brown.
8. Store the cookies in an airtight container in the fridge, or freeze them for later.

**Nutritions:** *Calories: 192, Total fat: 6g, Carbs: 34g, Fiber: 4g, Protein: 4g*

# 11. SUNSHINE MUFFINS

## INGREDIENTS

- 1 teaspoon coconut oil, for greasing muffin tins (optional)
- 2 tablespoons almond butter, or sunflower seed butter
- ¼ cup non-dairy milk
- 1 orange, peeled
- 1 carrot, coarsely chopped
- 2 tablespoons chopped dried apricots, or other dried fruit
- 3 tablespoons molasses
- 2 tablespoons ground flaxseed
- 1 teaspoon apple cider vinegar
- 1 teaspoon pure vanilla extract
- ½ teaspoon ground cinnamon
- ½ teaspoon ground ginger (optional)
- ¼ teaspoon ground nutmeg (optional)
- ¼ teaspoon allspice (optional)
- ¾ cup rolled oats, or whole-grain flour
- 1 teaspoon baking powder
- ½ teaspoon baking soda

## DIRECTIONS

1. Preheat the oven to 350°F. Prepare a 6-cup muffin tin by rubbing the insides of the cups with coconut oil or using silicone or paper muffin cups.
2. Purée the nut butter, milk, orange, carrot, apricots, molasses, flaxseed, vinegar, vanilla, cinnamon, ginger, nutmeg, and allspice in a food processor or blender until somewhat smooth.
3. Grind the oats in a clean coffee grinder until they're the consistency of flour (or use whole-grain flour). In a large bowl, mix the oats with the baking powder and baking soda.
4. Mix the wet ingredients into the dry ingredients until just combined. Fold in the mix-ins (if using).
5. Spoon about ¼ cup batter into each muffin cup and bake for 30 minutes, or until a toothpick inserted into the center comes out clean. The orange creates a very moist base, so the muffins may take longer than 30 minutes, depending on how heavy your muffin tin is.

**Nutritions:** *Calories: 287, Total fat: 12g, Carbs: 41g, Fiber: 6g, Protein: 8g*

# 12. APPLESAUCE CRUMBLE MUFFINS

## INGREDIENTS

- 1 teaspoon coconut oil, for greasing muffin tins (optional)
- 2 tablespoons nut butter, or seed butter
- 1½ cups unsweetened applesauce
- ⅓ cup coconut sugar
- ½ cup non-dairy milk
- 2 tablespoons ground flaxseed
- 1 teaspoon apple cider vinegar
- 1 teaspoon pure vanilla extract
- 2 cups whole-grain flour
- 1 teaspoon baking soda
- ½ teaspoon baking powder
- 1 teaspoon ground cinnamon
- Pinch sea salt
- ½ cup walnuts, chopped

## DIRECTIONS

1. Preheat the oven to 350°F. Prepare two 6-cup muffin tins by rubbing the insides of the cups with coconut oil, or using silicone or paper muffin cups.
2. In a large bowl, mix the nut butter, applesauce, coconut sugar, milk, flaxseed, vinegar, and vanilla until thoroughly combined, or purée in a food processor or blender.
3. In another large bowl, sift together the flour, baking soda, baking powder, cinnamon, salt, and chopped walnuts.
4. Mix the dry ingredients into the wet ingredients until just combined.
5. Spoon about ¼ cup batter into each muffin cup and sprinkle with the topping of your choice (if using). Bake for 15 to 20 minutes, or until a toothpick inserted into the center comes out clean. The applesauce creates a very moist base, so the muffins may take longer, depending on how heavy your muffin tins are.

**Nutritions:** *Calories: 287, Total fat: 12g, Carbs: 41g, Fiber: 6g, Protein: 8g*

# 13. BAKED BANANA FRENCH TOAST WITH RASPBERRY SYRUP

## INGREDIENTS

**FOR THE FRENCH TOAST**
- 1 banana
- 1 cup coconut milk
- 1 teaspoon pure vanilla extract
- ¼ teaspoon ground nutmeg
- ½ teaspoon ground cinnamon
- 1½ teaspoons arrowroot powder, or flour
- Pinch sea salt
- 8 slices whole-grain bread

**FOR THE RASPBERRY SYRUP**
- 1 cup fresh or frozen raspberries, or other berries
- 2 tablespoons water, or pure fruit juice
- 1 to 2 tablespoons maple syrup, or coconut sugar (optional)

## DIRECTIONS

**TO MAKE THE FRENCH TOAST**
1. Preheat the oven to 350°F.
2. In a shallow bowl, purée or mash the banana well. Mix in the coconut milk, vanilla, nutmeg, cinnamon, arrowroot, and salt.
3. Dip the slices of bread in the banana mixture, and then lay them out in a 13-by-9-inch baking dish. They should cover the bottom of the dish and can overlap a bit but shouldn't be stacked on top of each other. Pour any leftover banana mixture over the bread, and put the dish in the oven. Bake about 30 minutes, or until the tops are lightly browned.
4. Serve topped with raspberry syrup.

**TO MAKE THE RASPBERRY SYRUP**
5. Heat the raspberries in a small pot with the water and the maple syrup (if using) on medium heat.
6. Leave to simmer, stirring occasionally and breaking up the berries, for 15 to 20 minutes, until the liquid has reduced.

**Nutritions:** *Calories: 166, Total fat: 7g, Carbs: 23g, Fiber: 4g, Protein: 5g*

# CHAPTER 8:
# SMOOTHIES AND BREAKFASTS RECIPES PART 2

# 14. CINNAMON APPLE TOAST

## INGREDIENTS

- 1 to 2 teaspoons coconut oil
- ½ teaspoon ground cinnamon
- 1 tablespoon maple syrup, or coconut sugar
- 1 apple, cored and thinly sliced
- 2 slices whole-grain bread

## DIRECTIONS

1. In a large bowl, mix the coconut oil, cinnamon, and maple syrup together. Add the apple slices and toss with your hands to coat them.
2. To panfry the toast, place the apple slices in a medium skillet on medium-high and cook for about 5 minutes, or until slightly soft, then transfer to a plate. Cook the bread in the same skillet for 2 to 3 minutes on each side. Top the toast with the apples. Alternately, you can bake the toast. Use your hands to rub each slice of bread with some of the coconut oil mixture on both sides. Lay them on a small baking sheet, top with the coated apples, and put in the oven or toaster oven at 350°F for 15 to 20 minutes, or until the apples have softened.

**Nutritions:** *Calories: 187, Total fat: 8g, Carbs: 27g, Fiber: 4g, Protein: 4g*

# 15. MUESLI AND BERRIES BOWL

## INGREDIENTS

**FOR THE MUESLI**
- 1 cup rolled oats
- 1 cup spelt flakes, or quinoa flakes, or more rolled oats
- 2 cups puffed cereal
- ¼ cup sunflower seeds
- ¼ cup almonds
- ¼ cup raisins
- ¼ cup dried cranberries
- ¼ cup chopped dried figs
- ¼ cup unsweetened shredded coconut
- ¼ cup non-dairy chocolate chips
- 1 to 3 teaspoons ground cinnamon

**FOR THE BOWL**
- ½ cup non-dairy milk, or unsweetened applesauce
- ¾ cup muesli
- ½ cup berries

## DIRECTIONS

1. Put the muesli ingredients in a container or bag and shake.
2. Combine the muesli and bowl ingredients in a bowl or to-go container.

**Nutritions:** *Calories: 441, Total fat: 20g, Carbs: 63g, Fiber: 13g, Protein: 10g*

# 16. WHOLE-WHEAT BLUEBERRY MUFFINS

## INGREDIENTS

- ½ cup plant-based milk
- ½ cup unsweetened applesauce
- ½ cup maple syrup
- 1 teaspoon vanilla extract
- 2 cups whole-wheat flour
- ½ teaspoon baking soda
- 1 cup blueberries

## DIRECTIONS

1. Preheat the oven to 375°F.
2. In a large bowl, mix together the milk, applesauce, maple syrup, and vanilla.
3. Stir in the flour and baking soda until no dry flour is left and the batter is smooth.
4. Gently fold in the blueberries until they are evenly distributed throughout the batter.
5. In a muffin tin, fill 8 muffin cups three-quarters full of batter.
6. Bake for 25 minutes, or until you can stick a knife into the center of a muffin and it comes out clean. Allow to cool before serving.

**Preparation Tip**: Both frozen and fresh blueberries will work great in this recipe. The only difference will be that muffins using fresh blueberries will cook slightly quicker than those using frozen.

**Nutritions:** *Calories: 200, Total fat: 1g, Carbohydrates: 45g, Fiber: 2g, Protein: 4g*

# 17. WALNUT CRUNCH BANANA BREAD

## INGREDIENTS

- 4 ripe bananas
- ¼ cup maple syrup
- 1 tablespoon apple cider vinegar
- 1 teaspoon vanilla extract
- 1½ cups whole-wheat flour
- ½ teaspoon ground cinnamon
- ½ teaspoon baking soda
- ¼ cup walnut pieces (optional)

## DIRECTIONS

1. Preheat the oven to 350°F.
2. In a large bowl, use a fork or mixing spoon to mash the bananas until they reach a puréed consistency (small bits of banana are fine). Stir in the maple syrup, apple cider vinegar, and vanilla.
3. Stir in the flour, cinnamon, and baking soda. Fold in the walnut pieces (if using).
4. Gently pour the batter into a loaf pan, filling it no more than three-quarters of the way full. Bake for 1 hour, or until you can stick a knife into the middle and it comes out clean.
5. Remove from the oven and allow to cool on the countertop for a minimum of 30 minutes before serving.

**Nutritions:** *Calories: 178, Total fat: 1g, Carbohydrates: 40g, Fiber: 5g, Protein: 4g*

# 18. PLANT-POWERED PANCAKES

## INGREDIENTS

- 1 cup whole-wheat flour
- 1 teaspoon baking powder
- ½ teaspoon ground cinnamon
- 1 cup plant-based milk
- ½ cup unsweetened applesauce
- ¼ cup maple syrup
- 1 teaspoon vanilla extract

## DIRECTIONS

1. In a large bowl, combine the flour, baking powder, and cinnamon.
2. Stir in the milk, applesauce, maple syrup, and vanilla until no dry flour is left and the batter is smooth.
3. Heat a large, nonstick skillet or griddle over medium heat. For each pancake, pour ¼ cup of batter onto the hot skillet. Once bubbles form over the top of the pancake and the sides begin to brown, flip and cook for 1 to 2 minutes more.
4. Repeat until all of the batter is used, and serve.

**Nutritions:** *Calories: 210, Total fat: 2g, Carbohydrates: 44g, Fiber: 5g, Protein: 5g*

PREPARATION: 5 MIN      COOKING: 50 MIN      SERVES: 4

# 19. MAPLE-PECAN GRANOLA

## INGREDIENTS

- 1½ cups rolled oats
- ¼ cup pecan pieces
- ¼ cup maple syrup
- 1 teaspoon vanilla extract
- ½ teaspoon ground cinnamon

## DIRECTIONS

1. Preheat the oven to 300°F. Line a baking sheet with parchment paper.
2. In a large bowl, combine the oats, pecan pieces, maple syrup, vanilla, and cinnamon. Stir until the oats and pecan pieces are completely coated.
3. Spread the mixture on the baking sheet in an even layer. Bake for 20 minutes, stirring once after 10 minutes.
4. Remove from the oven, and allow to cool on the countertop for 30 minutes before serving. The granola may still be a bit soft right after you remove it from the oven, but it will gradually firm up as it cools.

**Nutritions:** *Calories: 220, Total fat: 7g, Carbohydrates: 35g, Fiber: 4g, Protein: 5g*

# 20. PARADISE ISLAND OVERNIGHT OATMEAL

## INGREDIENTS

- 2 cups rolled oats
- 2 cups plant-based milk
- ½ cup diced mango (fresh or frozen)
- ½ cup pineapple chunks (fresh or frozen)
- 1 banana, sliced
- 1 tablespoon maple syrup
- 1 tablespoon chia seeds

## DIRECTIONS

1. In a large bowl, mix together the oats, milk, mango, pineapple, banana, maple syrup, and chia seeds.
2. Cover and refrigerate overnight or for a minimum of 4 hours before serving.

**Nutritions:** *Calories: 510, Total fat: 12g, Carbohydrates: 93g, Fiber: 15g, Protein: 14g*

# 21. PUMPKIN PIE OATMEAL

## INGREDIENTS

- 3 cups plant-based milk
- 1 cup steel-cut oats
- 1 cup unsweetened pumpkin purée
- 2 tablespoons maple syrup
- 1 teaspoon ground cinnamon
- ⅛ teaspoon ground cloves
- ⅛ teaspoon ground nutmeg

## DIRECTIONS

1. In a medium saucepan over medium-high heat, bring the milk to a boil. When a rolling boil is reached, reduce the heat to low, and stir in the oats, pumpkin purée, maple syrup, cinnamon, cloves, and nutmeg.
2. Cover and cook for 30 minutes, stirring every few minutes to ensure none of the oatmeal sticks to the bottom of the pot, and serve.

**Nutritions:** *Calories: 218, Total fat: 5g, Carbohydrates: 38g, Fiber: 6g, Protein: 7g*

# 22. CHOCOLATE AND PEANUT BUTTER QUINOA

## INGREDIENTS

- 1 cup plant-based milk (here or here)
- 2 cups cooked quinoa (see here)
- 1 tablespoon maple syrup
- 1 tablespoon cocoa powder
- 1 tablespoon defatted peanut powder

## DIRECTIONS

1. In a medium saucepan over medium-high heat, bring the milk to a boil.
2. Once a rolling boil is reached, reduce the heat to low, and stir in the quinoa, maple syrup, cocoa powder, and peanut powder.
3. Cook, uncovered, for 5 minutes, stirring every other minute. Serve warm.

**Nutritions:** *Calories: 339, Total fat: 8g, Carbohydrates: 53g, Fiber: 7g, Protein: 14g*

# 23. A.M. BREAKFAST SCRAMBLE

## INGREDIENTS

- 1 (14-ounce) package firm or extra-firm tofu
- 4 ounces mushrooms, sliced
- ½ bell pepper, diced
- 2 tablespoons nutritional yeast
- 1 tablespoon vegetable broth or water
- ½ teaspoon garlic powder
- ½ teaspoon onion powder
- ⅛ teaspoon freshly ground black pepper
- 1 cup fresh spinach

## DIRECTIONS

1. Heat a large skillet over medium-low heat.
2. Drain the tofu, then place it in the skillet and mash it down with a fork or mixing spoon. Stir in the mushrooms, bell pepper, nutritional yeast, broth, garlic powder, onion powder, and pepper. Cover and cook for 10 minutes, stirring once after about 5 minutes.
3. Uncover, and stir in the spinach. Cook for an additional 5 minutes before serving.

**Nutritions:** *Calories: 230, Total fat: 10g, Carbohydrates: 16g, Fiber: 7g, Protein: 27g*

# 24. LOADED BREAKFAST BURRITO

## INGREDIENTS

- ½ block (7 ounces) firm tofu
- 2 medium potatoes, cut into ¼-inch dice
- 1 cup cooked black beans, drained and rinsed
- 4 ounces mushrooms, sliced
- 1 jalapeño, seeded and diced
- 2 tablespoons vegetable broth or water
- 1 tablespoon nutritional yeast
- ½ teaspoon garlic powder
- ½ teaspoon onion powder
- ¼ cup salsa
- 6 corn tortillas

## DIRECTIONS

1. Heat a large skillet over medium-low heat.
2. Drain the tofu, then place it in the pan and mash it down with a fork or mixing spoon.
3. Stir the potatoes, black beans, mushrooms, jalapeño, broth, nutritional yeast, garlic powder, and onion powder into the skillet. Reduce the heat to low, cover, and cook for 10 minutes, or until the potatoes can be easily pierced with a fork.
4. Uncover, and stir in the salsa. Cook for 5 minutes, stirring every other minute.
5. Warm the tortillas in a microwave for 15 to 30 seconds or in a warm oven until soft.
6. Remove the pan from the heat, place one-sixth of the filling in the center of each tortilla, and roll the tortillas into burritos before serving.

**Nutritions:** *Calories: 535, Total fat: 8g, Carbohydrates: 95g, Fiber: 21g, Protein: 29g*

# 25. SOUTHWEST SWEET POTATO SKILLET

## INGREDIENTS

- 4 medium sweet potatoes, cut into ½-inch dice
- 8 ounces mushrooms, sliced
- 1 bell pepper, diced
- 1 sweet onion, diced
- 1 cup vegetable broth or water, plus 1 to 2 tablespoons more if needed
- 1 teaspoon garlic powder
- ½ teaspoon ground cumin
- ½ teaspoon chili powder
- ⅛ teaspoon freshly ground black pepper

## DIRECTIONS

1. Heat a large skillet over medium-low heat.
2. When the skillet is hot, put the sweet potatoes, mushrooms, bell pepper, onion, broth, garlic powder, cumin, chili powder, and pepper in it and stir. Cover and cook for 10 minutes, or until the sweet potatoes are easily pierced with a fork.
3. Uncover, and give the mixture a good stir. (If any of the contents are beginning to stick to the bottom of the pan, add 1 to 2 tablespoons of broth.)
4. Cook, uncovered, for an additional 5 minutes, stirring once after about 2½ minutes, and serve.

**Nutritions:** *Calories: 158, Total fat: 1g, Carbohydrates: 34g, Fiber: 6g, Protein: 6g*

# CHAPTER 9:
# SOUP AND STEWS RECIPES

# 26. LIME-MINT SOUP

## INGREDIENTS

- 4 cups vegetable broth
- ¼ cup fresh mint leaves, roughly chopped
- ¼ cup chopped scallions, white and green parts
- 3 garlic cloves, minced
- 3 tablespoons freshly squeezed lime juice

## DIRECTIONS

1. In a large stockpot, combine the broth, mint, scallions, garlic, and lime juice. Bring to a boil over medium-high heat.
2. 2.Cover, reduce the heat to low, simmer for 15 minutes, and serve.

**Nutritions:** *Calories: 55, Total fat: 2g, Carbohydrates: 5g, Fiber: 1g, Protein: 5g*

# 27. SAVORY SPLIT PEA SOUP

## INGREDIENTS

- 1 (16-ounce) package dried green split peas, soaked overnight
- 5 cups vegetable broth or water
- 2 teaspoons garlic powder
- 2 teaspoons onion powder
- 1 teaspoon dried oregano
- 1 teaspoon dried thyme
- ¼ teaspoon freshly ground black pepper

## DIRECTIONS

1. overnight to soak
2. In a large stockpot, combine the split peas, broth, garlic powder, onion powder, oregano, thyme, and pepper. Bring to a boil over medium-high heat.
3. 2.Cover, reduce the heat to medium-low, and simmer for 45 minutes, stirring every 5 to 10 minutes. Serve warm.

**Nutritions:** *Calories: 297, Total fat: 2g, Carbohydrates: 48g, Fiber: 20g, Protein: 23g*

# 28. KALE AND LENTIL STEW

## INGREDIENTS

- 5 cups (2 pounds) brown or green dry lentils
- 8 cups vegetable broth or water
- 4 cups kale, stemmed and chopped into 2-inch pieces
- 2 large carrots, diced
- 1 tablespoon smoked paprika
- 2 teaspoons onion powder
- 2 teaspoons garlic powder
- 1 teaspoon red pepper flakes
- 1 teaspoon dried oregano
- 1 teaspoon dried thyme

## DIRECTIONS

1. In a large stockpot, combine the lentils, broth, kale, carrots, paprika, onion powder, garlic powder, red pepper flakes, oregano, and thyme. Bring to a boil over medium-high heat.
2. Cover, reduce the heat to medium-low, and simmer for 45 minutes, stirring every 5 to 10 minutes. Serve warm.

**Nutritions:** *Calories: 467, Total fat: 3g, Carbohydrates: 78g, Fiber: 31g, Protein: 32g*

# 29. FOUR-CAN CHILI

## INGREDIENTS

- 1 (28-ounce) can crushed tomatoes
- 1 (15-ounce) can low-sodium black beans
- 1 (15-ounce) can low-sodium cannellini beans
- 1 (15-ounce) can low-sodium chickpeas
- 1 tablespoon chili powder
- 1 teaspoon garlic powder
- 1 teaspoon onion powder
- ½ teaspoon ground cumin
- ½ teaspoon red pepper flakes (optional)

## DIRECTIONS

1. In a large stockpot, combine the tomatoes, black beans, cannellini beans, and chickpeas and their liquids with the chili powder, garlic powder, onion powder, cumin, and red pepper flakes (if using). Bring the chili to a boil over medium-high heat.
2. 2.Cover, reduce the heat to medium-low, simmer for 25 minutes, and serve.

**Nutritions:** *Calories: 185, Total fat: 1g, Carbohydrates: 33g, Fiber: 13g, Protein: 11g*

# 30. SAUTÉED COLLARD GREENS

## INGREDIENTS

- 1½ pounds collard greens
- 1 cup vegetable broth
- ½ teaspoon garlic powder
- ½ teaspoon onion powder
- ⅛ teaspoon freshly ground black pepper

## DIRECTIONS

1. Remove the hard-middle stems from the greens, then roughly chop the leaves into 2-inch pieces.
2. In a large saucepan, mix together the vegetable broth, garlic powder, onion powder, and pepper. Bring to a boil over medium-high heat, then add the chopped greens. Reduce the heat to low, and cover.
3. Cook for 20 minutes, stirring well every 4 to 5 minutes, and serve. (If you notice that the liquid has completely evaporated and the greens are beginning to stick to the bottom of the pan, stir in a few extra tablespoons of vegetable broth or water.)

**Nutritions:** *Calories: 28, Total fat: 1g, Carbohydrates: 4g, Fiber: 2g, Protein: 3g*

# 31. CREAM OF MUSHROOM SOUP

## INGREDIENTS

- 1 medium white onion, peeled, chopped
- 16 ounces button mushrooms, sliced
- 1 ½ teaspoon minced garlic
- 1/4 cup all-purpose flour
- 1/2 teaspoon ground black pepper
- 1 teaspoon dried thyme
- 1/4 teaspoon nutmeg
- 1/2 teaspoon salt
- 2 tablespoons vegan butter
- 4 cups vegetable broth
- 1 1/2 cups coconut milk, unsweetened

## DIRECTIONS

1. Take a large pot, place it over medium-high heat, add butter and when it melts, add onions and garlic, stir in garlic and cook for 5 minutes until softened and nicely brown.
2. Then sprinkle flour over vegetables, continue cooking for 1 minute, then add remaining ingredients, stir until mixed and simmer for 5 minutes until thickened.
3. Serve straight away

**Nutritions:** *Calories: 120 Cal, Fat: 7 g, Carbs: 10 g, Protein: 2 g, Fiber: 6 g*

# 32. CAULIFLOWER AND HORSERADISH SOUP

## INGREDIENTS

- 2 medium potatoes, peeled, chopped
- 1 medium cauliflower, florets and stalk chopped
- 1 medium white onion, peeled, chopped
- 1 teaspoon minced garlic
- 2/3 teaspoon salt
- 1/3 teaspoon ground black pepper
- 4 teaspoons horseradish sauce
- 1 teaspoon dried thyme
- 3 cups vegetable broth
- 1 cup coconut milk, unsweetened

## DIRECTIONS

1. Place all the vegetables in a large pan, place it over medium-high heat, add thyme, pour in broth and milk and bring the mixture to boil.
2. Then switch heat to medium level, simmer the soup for 15 minutes and remove the pan from heat.
3. Puree the soup by using an immersion blender until smooth, season with salt and black pepper, and serve straight away.

**Nutritions:** *Calories: 160 Cal, Fat: 2.6 g, Carbs: 31 g, Protein: 6 g, Fiber: 6 g*

# 33. CURRY LENTIL SOUP

## INGREDIENTS

- 1 cup brown lentils
- 1 medium white onion, peeled, chopped
- 28 ounces diced tomatoes
- 1 ½ teaspoon minced garlic
- 1 inch of ginger, grated
- 3 cups vegetable broth
- 1/2 teaspoon salt
- 2 tablespoons curry powder
- 1 teaspoon cumin
- 1/2 teaspoon cayenne
- 1 tablespoon olive oil
- 1 1/2 cups coconut milk, unsweetened
- ¼ cup chopped cilantro

## DIRECTIONS

1. Take a soup pot, place it over medium-high heat, add oil and when hot, add onion, stir in garlic and ginger and cook for 5 minutes until golden brown.
2. Then add all the ingredients except for milk and cilantro, stir until mixed and simmer for 25 minutes until lentils have cooked.
3. When done, stir in milk, cook for 5 minutes until thoroughly heated and then garnish the soup with cilantro.
4. Serve straight away

**Nutritions:** *Calories: 269 Cal, Fat: 15 g, Carbs: 26 g, Protein: 10 g, Fiber: 10 g*

# 34. CHICKPEA NOODLE SOUP

## INGREDIENTS

- 1 cup cooked chickpeas
- 8 ounces rotini noodles, whole-wheat
- 4 celery stalks, sliced
- 2 medium white onions, peeled, chopped
- 4 medium carrots, peeled, sliced
- 2 teaspoons minced garlic
- 8 sprigs of thyme
- 1 teaspoon salt
- 1/3 teaspoon ground black pepper
- 1 bay leaf
- 2 tablespoons olive oil
- 2 quarts of vegetable broth
- ¼ cup chopped fresh parsley

## DIRECTIONS

1. Take a large pot, place it over medium heat, add oil and when hot, add all the vegetables, stir in garlic, thyme and bay leaf and cook for 5 minutes until vegetables are golden and sauté.
2. Then pour in broth stir and bring the mixture to boil.
3. Add chickpeas and noodles into boiling soup, continue cooking for 8 minutes until noodles are tender, and then season soup with salt and black pepper.
4. Garnish with parsley and serve straight away

**Nutritions:** *Calories: 260 Cal, Fat: 5 g, Carbs: 44 g, Protein: 7 g, Fiber: 4 g*

# 35. MEXICAN LENTIL SOUP

## INGREDIENTS

- 2 cups green lentils
- 1 medium red bell pepper, cored, diced
- 1 medium white onion, peeled, diced
- 2 cups diced tomatoes
- 8 ounces diced green chilies
- 2 celery stalks, diced
- 2 medium carrots, peeled, diced
- 1 ½ teaspoon minced garlic
- 1/2 teaspoon salt
- 1 tablespoon cumin
- 1/4 teaspoon smoked paprika
- 1 teaspoon oregano
- 1/8 teaspoon hot sauce
- 2 tablespoons olive oil
- 8 cups vegetable broth
- ¼ cup cilantro, for garnish
- 1 avocado, peeled, pitted, diced, for garnish

## DIRECTIONS

1. Take a large pot over medium heat, add oil and when hot, add all the vegetables, reserving tomatoes and chilies, and cook for 5 minutes until softened.
2. Then add garlic, stir in oregano, cumin, and paprika, and continue cooking for 1 minute.
3. Add lentils, tomatoes and green chilies, season with salt, pour in the broth and simmer the soup for 40 minutes until cooked.
4. When done, ladle soup into bowls, top with avocado and cilantro and serve straight away

**Nutritions:** *Calories: 235 Cal, Fat: 9 g, Carbs: 32 g, Protein: 9 g, Fiber: 10 g*

# 36. PORTOBELLO MUSHROOM STEW

## INGREDIENTS

- 8 cups vegetable broth
- 1 cup dried wild mushrooms
- 1 cup dried chickpeas
- 3 cups chopped potato
- 2 cups chopped carrots
- 1 cup corn kernels
- 2 cups diced white onions
- 1 tablespoon minced parsley
- 3 cups chopped zucchini
- 1 tablespoon minced rosemary
- 1 1/2 teaspoon ground black pepper
- 1 teaspoon dried sage
- 2/3 teaspoon salt
- 1 teaspoon dried oregano
- 3 tablespoons soy sauce
- 1 1/2 teaspoons liquid smoke
- 8 ounces tomato paste

## DIRECTIONS

1. Switch on the slow cooker, add all the ingredients in it, and stir until mixed.
2. Shut the cooker with lid and cook for 10 hours at a high heat setting until cooked.
3. Serve straight away.

**Nutritions:** *Calories: 447 Cal, Fat: 36 g, Carbs: 24 g, Protein: 11 g, Fiber: 2 g*

# 37. ROOT VEGETABLE STEW

## INGREDIENTS

- 2 cups chopped kale
- 1 large white onion, peeled, chopped
- 1-pound parsnips, peeled, chopped
- 1-pound potatoes, peeled, chopped
- 2 celery ribs, chopped
- 1-pound butternut squash, peeled, deseeded, chopped
- 1-pound carrots, peeled, chopped
- 3 teaspoons minced garlic
- 1-pound sweet potatoes, peeled, chopped
- 1 bay leaf
- 1 teaspoon ground black pepper
- 1/2 teaspoon sea salt
- 1 tablespoon chopped sage
- 3 cups vegetable broth

## DIRECTIONS

1. Switch on the slow cooker, add all the ingredients in it, except for the kale, and stir until mixed.
2. Shut the cooker with lid and cook for 8 hours at a low heat setting until cooked.
3. When done, add kale into the stew, stir until mixed, and cook for 10 minutes until leaves have wilted.
4. Serve straight away.

**Nutritions:** *Calories: 120 Cal, Fat: 1 g, Carbs: 28 g, Protein: 4 g, Fiber: 6 g*

# 38. BLACK BEAN AND QUINOA STEW

## INGREDIENTS

- 1-pound black beans, dried, soaked overnight
- 3/4 cup quinoa, uncooked
- 1 medium red bell pepper, cored, chopped
- 1 medium red onion, peeled, diced
- 1 medium green bell pepper, cored, chopped
- 28-ounce diced tomatoes
- 2 dried chipotle peppers
- 1 ½ teaspoon minced garlic
- 2/3 teaspoon sea salt
- 2 teaspoons red chili powder
- 1/3 teaspoon ground black pepper
- 1 teaspoon coriander powder
- 1 dried cinnamon stick
- 1/4 cup cilantro
- 7 cups of water

## DIRECTIONS

1. Switch on the slow cooker, add all the ingredients in it, except for salt, and stir until mixed.
2. Shut the cooker with lid and cook for 6 hours at a high heat setting until cooked.
3. When done, stir salt into the stew until mixed, remove cinnamon sticks and serve.

**Nutritions:** *Calories: 308 Cal, Fat: 2 g, Carbs: 70 g, Protein: 23 g, Fiber: 32 g*

# CHAPTER 10:
# SOUP AND STEWS RECIPES PART 2

# 39. VEGETARIAN GUMBO

## INGREDIENTS

- 1 1/2 cups diced zucchini
- 16-ounces cooked red beans
- 4 cups sliced okra
- 1 1/2 cups diced green pepper
- 1 1/2 cups chopped white onion
- 1 1/2 cups diced red bell pepper
- 8 cremini mushrooms, quartered
- 1 cup sliced celery
- 3 teaspoons minced garlic
- 1 medium tomato, chopped
- 1 teaspoon red pepper flakes
- 1 teaspoon dried thyme
- 3 tablespoons all-purpose flour
- 1 tablespoon smoked paprika
- 1 teaspoon dried oregano
- 1/4 teaspoon nutmeg
- 1 teaspoon soy sauce
- 1 1/2 teaspoons liquid smoke
- 2 tablespoons mustard
- 1 tablespoon apple cider vinegar
- 1 tablespoon Worcestershire sauce, vegetarian
- 1/2 teaspoon hot sauce
- 3 tablespoons olive oil
- 4 cups vegetable stock
- 1/2 cups sliced green onion
- 4 cups cooked jasmine rice

## DIRECTIONS

1. Take a Dutch oven, place it over medium heat, add oil and flour and cook for 5 minutes until fragrant.
2. Switch heat to the medium low level, and continue cooking for 20 minutes until roux becomes dark brown, whisking constantly.
3. Meanwhile, place the tomato in a food processor, add garlic and onion along with remaining ingredients, except for stock, zucchini, celery, mushroom, green and red bell pepper, and pulse for 2 minutes until smooth.
4. Pour the mixture into the pan, return pan over medium-high heat, stir until mixed, and cook for 5 minutes until all the liquid has evaporated.
5. Stir in stock, bring it to simmer, then add remaining vegetables and simmer for 20 minutes until tender.
6. Garnish gumbo with green onions and serve with rice.

**Nutritions:** *Calories: 160 Cal, Fat: 7.3 g, Carbs: 20 g, Protein: 7 g, Fiber: 5.7 g*

# 40. BRUSSELS SPROUTS STEW

## INGREDIENTS

- 35 ounces Brussels sprouts
- 5 medium potato, peeled, chopped
- 1 medium onion, peeled, chopped
- 2 carrot, peeled, cubed
- 2 teaspoons smoked paprika
- 1/8 teaspoon ground black pepper
- 1/8 teaspoon salt
- 3 tablespoons caraway seeds
- 1/2 teaspoon red chili powder
- 1 tablespoon nutmeg
- 1 tablespoon olive oil
- 4 ½ cups hot vegetable stock

## DIRECTIONS

1. Take a large pot, place it over medium-high heat, add oil and when hot, add onion and cook for 1 minute.
2. Then add carrot and potato, cook for 2 minutes, then add Brussel sprouts and cook for 5 minutes.
3. Stir in all the spices, pour in vegetable stock, bring the mixture to boil, switch heat to medium-low and simmer for 45 minutes until cooked and stew reach to desired thickness.
4. Serve straight away.

**Nutritions:** *Calories: 156 Cal, Fat: 3 g, Carbs: 22 g, Protein: 12 g, Fiber: 5.1100 g*

# 41. SPINACH SOUP WITH DILL AND BASIL

## INGREDIENTS

- 1-pound peeled and diced potatoes
- 1 tablespoon minced garlic
- 1 teaspoon dry mustard
- 6 cups vegetable broth
- 20 ounces chopped frozen spinach
- 2 cups chopped onion
- 1 ½ tablespoons salt
- ½ cup minced dill
- 1 cup basil
- ½ teaspoon ground black pepper

## DIRECTIONS

1. Whisk onion, garlic, potatoes, broth, mustard, and salt in a pan cook it over medium flame. When it starts boiling, low down the heat and cover it with the lid and cook for 20 minutes. Add the remaining ingredients in it and blend it and cook it for few more minutes and serve it.

**Nutritions:** *Carbohydrates 12g, Protein 13g, Fats 1g, Calories 165.*

# 42. COCONUT WATERCRESS SOUP

## INGREDIENTS

- 1 teaspoon coconut oil
- 1 onion, diced
- ¾ cup coconut milk

## DIRECTIONS

1. Preparing the ingredients.
2. Melt the coconut oil in a large pot over medium-high heat. Add the onion and cook until soft, about 5 minutes, then add the peas and the water. Bring to a boil, then lower the heat and add the watercress, mint, salt, and pepper.
3. Cover and simmer for 5 minutes. Stir in the coconut milk, and purée the soup until smooth in a blender or with an immersion blender.
4. Try this soup with any other fresh, leafy green—anything from spinach to collard greens to arugula to Swiss chard.

**Nutritions:** *Calories: 178, Protein: 6g, Total fat: 10g, Carbohydrates: 18g, Fiber: 5g*

# 43. ROASTED RED PEPPER AND BUTTERNUT SQUASH SOUP

## INGREDIENTS

- 1 small butternut squash
- 1 tablespoon olive oil
- 1 teaspoon sea salt
- 2 red bell peppers
- 1 yellow onion
- 1 head garlic
- 2 cups water, or vegetable broth
- Zest and juice of 1 lime
- 1 to 2 tablespoons tahini
- Pinch cayenne pepper
- ½ teaspoon ground coriander
- ½ teaspoon ground cumin
- Toasted squash seeds (optional)

## DIRECTIONS

1. Preparing the ingredients.
2. Preheat the oven to 350°f.
3. Prepare the squash for roasting by cutting it in half lengthwise, scooping out the seeds, and poking some holes in the flesh with a fork. Reserve the seeds if desired.
4. Rub a small amount of oil over the flesh and skin, then rub with a bit of sea salt and put the halves skin-side down in a large baking dish. Put it in the oven while you prepare the rest of the vegetables.
5. Prepare the peppers the exact same way, except they do not need to be poked.
6. Slice the onion in half and rub oil on the exposed faces. Slice the top off the head of garlic and rub oil on the exposed flesh.
7. After the squash has cooked for 20 minutes, add the peppers, onion, and garlic, and roast for another 20 minutes. Optionally, you can toast the squash seeds by putting them in the oven in a separate baking dish 10 to 15 minutes before the vegetables are finished.
8. Keep a close eye on them. When the vegetables are cooked, take them out and let them cool before handling them. The squash will be very soft when poked with a fork.
9. Scoop the flesh out of the squash skin into a large pot (if you have an immersion blender) or into a blender.
10. Chop the pepper roughly, remove the onion skin and chop the onion roughly, and squeeze the garlic cloves out of the head, all into the pot or blender. Add the water, the lime zest and juice, and the tahini. Purée the soup, adding more water if you like, to your desired consistency. Season with the salt, cayenne, coriander, and cumin. Serve garnished with toasted squash seeds (if using).

**Nutritions:** *Calories: 156, Protein: 4g, Total fat: 7g, Saturated fat: 11g, Carbohydrates: 22g, Fiber: 5g*

# 44. TOMATO PUMPKIN SOUP

## INGREDIENTS

- 2 cups pumpkin, diced
- 1/2 cup tomato, chopped
- 1/2 cup onion, chopped
- 1 1/2 tsp curry powder
- 1/2 tsp paprika
- 2 cups vegetable stock
- 1 tsp olive oil
- 1/2 tsp garlic, minced

## DIRECTIONS

1. In a saucepan, add oil, garlic, and onion and sauté for 3 minutes over medium heat.
2. Add remaining ingredients into the saucepan and bring to boil.
3. Reduce heat and cover and simmer for 10 minutes.
4. Puree the soup using a blender until smooth.
5. Stir well and serve warm.

**Nutritions:** *Calories 70, Fat 2.7 g, Carbohydrates 13.8 g, Sugar 6.3 g, Protein 1.9 g, Cholesterol 0 mg*

# 45. CAULIFLOWER SPINACH SOUP

## INGREDIENTS

- 1/2 cup unsweetened coconut milk
- 5 oz fresh spinach, chopped
- 5 watercress, chopped
- 8 cups vegetable stock
- 1 lb cauliflower, chopped
- Salt

## DIRECTIONS

1. Add stock and cauliflower in a large saucepan and bring to boil over medium heat for 15 minutes.
2. Add spinach and watercress and cook for another 10 minutes.
3. Remove from heat and puree the soup using a blender until smooth.
4. Add coconut milk and stir well. Season with salt.
5. Stir well and serve hot.

**Nutritions:** *Calories 153, Fat 8.3 g, Carbohydrates 8.7 g, Sugar 4.3 g, Protein 11.9 g, Cholesterol 0 mg*

# 46. AVOCADO MINT SOUP

## INGREDIENTS

- 1 medium avocado, peeled, pitted, and cut into pieces
- 1 cup coconut milk
- 2 romaine lettuce leaves
- 20 fresh mint leaves
- 1 tbsp fresh lime juice
- 1/8 tsp salt

## DIRECTIONS

1. Add all ingredients into the blender and blend until smooth. Soup should be thick not as a puree.
2. Pour into the serving bowls and place in the refrigerator for 10 minutes.
3. Stir well and serve chilled.

**Nutritions:** *Calories 268, Fat 25.6 g, Carbohydrates 10.2 g, Sugar 0.6 g, Protein 2.7, Cholesterol 0 mg*

# 47. CREAMY SQUASH SOUP

## INGREDIENTS

- 3 cups butternut squash, chopped
- 1 ½ cups unsweetened coconut milk
- 1 tbsp coconut oil
- 1 tsp dried onion flakes
- 1 tbsp curry powder
- 4 cups water
- 1 garlic clove
- 1 tsp kosher salt

## DIRECTIONS

1. Add squash, coconut oil, onion flakes, curry powder, water, garlic, and salt into a large saucepan. Bring to boil over high heat.
2. Turn heat to medium and simmer for 20 minutes.
3. Puree the soup using a blender until smooth. Return soup to the saucepan and stir in coconut milk and cook for 2 minutes.
4. Stir well and serve hot.

**Nutritions:** *Calories 146, Fat 12.6 g, Carbohydrates 9.4 g, Sugar 2.8 g, Protein 1.7 g, Cholesterol 0 mg*

# 48. ZUCCHINI SOUP

## INGREDIENTS

- 2 ½ lbs. zucchini, peeled and sliced
- 1/3 cup basil leaves
- 4 cups vegetable stock
- 4 garlic cloves, chopped
- 2 tbsp olive oil
- 1 medium onion, diced
- Pepper
- Salt

## DIRECTIONS

1. Heat olive oil in a pan over medium-low heat.
2. Add zucchini and onion and sauté until softened. Add garlic and sauté for a minute.
3. Add vegetable stock and simmer for 15 minutes.
4. Remove from heat. Stir in basil and puree the soup using a blender until smooth and creamy. Season with pepper and salt.
5. Stir well and serve.

**Nutritions:** *Calories 130, Fat 11 g, Carbohydrates 9.4 g, Sugar 2.5 g, Protein 1.6 g, Cholesterol 0 mg*

# 49. CREAMY CELERY SOUP

## INGREDIENTS

- 6 cups celery
- ½ tsp dill
- 2 cups water
- 1 cup coconut milk
- 1 onion, chopped
- Pinch of salt

## DIRECTIONS

1. Add all ingredients into the electric pot and stir well.
2. Cover electric pot with the lid and select soup setting.
3. Release pressure using a quick release method than open the lid.
4. Puree the soup using an immersion blender until smooth and creamy.
5. Stir well and serve warm.

**Nutritions:** *Calories 130, Fat 11 g, Carbohydrates 9.4 g, Sugar 2.5 g, Protein 1.6 g, Cholesterol 0 mg*

# 50. AVOCADO CUCUMBER SOUP

## INGREDIENTS

- 1 large cucumber, peeled and sliced
- ¾ cup water
- ¼ cup lemon juice
- 2 garlic cloves
- 6 green onion
- 2 avocados, pitted
- ½ tsp black pepper
- ½ tsp pink salt

## DIRECTIONS

1. Add all ingredients into the blender and blend until smooth and creamy.
2. Place in refrigerator for 30 minutes.
3. Stir well and serve chilled.

**Nutritions:** *Calories 140, Fat 14 g, Carbohydrates 9.3 g, Sugar 2.4 g, Protein 1.7 g, Cholesterol 0 mg*

# 51. CREAMY GARLIC ONION SOUP

## INGREDIENTS

- 1 onion, sliced
- 4 cups vegetable stock
- 1 1/2 tbsp olive oil
- 1 shallot, sliced
- 2 garlic cloves, chopped
- 1 leek, sliced
- Salt

## DIRECTIONS

1. Add stock and olive oil in a saucepan and bring to boil.
2. Add remaining ingredients and stir well.
3. Cover and simmer for 25 minutes.
4. Puree the soup using an immersion blender until smooth.
5. Stir well and serve warm.

**Nutritions:** *Calories 130, Fat 11 g, Carbohydrates 9.2 g, Sugar 2.3 g, Protein 1.6 g, Cholesterol 0 mg*

# CHAPTER 11:
# SNACK AND SIDES RECIPES

# 52. CINNAMON BAKED APPLE CHIPS

## INGREDIENTS

- 1 teaspoon cinnamon
- 1-2 apples

## DIRECTIONS

1. Preheat your oven to 200 degrees Fahrenheit
2. Take a sharp knife and slice apples into thin slices
3. Discard seeds
4. Line a baking sheet with parchment paper and arrange apples on it
5. Make sure they do not overlap
6. Once done, sprinkle cinnamon over apples
7. Bake in the oven for 1 hour
8. Flip and bake for an hour more until no longer moist
9. Serve and enjoy!

**Nutritions:** *Calories: 147, Fat: 0g, Carbohydrates: 39g, Protein: 1g*

# 53. ACORN SQUASH WITH MANGO CHUTNEY

## INGREDIENTS

- 1 large acorn squash
- ¼ cup mango chutney
- ¼ cup flaked coconut
- Salt and pepper as needed

## DIRECTIONS

1. Cut the squash into quarters and remove the seeds, discard the stringy pulp.
2. Spray your cooker with olive oil.
3. Transfer the squash to the slow cooker
4. Take a bowl and add coconut and chutney, mix well and divide the mixture into the center of the Squash.
5. Season well.
6. Place lid on top and cook on LOW for 2-3 hours.
7. Enjoy!

**Nutritions:** *Calories: 226, Fat: 6g, Carbohydrates: 24g, Protein: 17g*

# 54. HEALTHY CARROT CHIPS

## INGREDIENTS

- 3 cups carrots, sliced into paper-thin rounds
- 2 tablespoons olive oil
- 2 teaspoons ground cumin
- ½ teaspoon smoked paprika
- Pinch of salt

## DIRECTIONS

1. Preheat your oven to 400 degrees Fahrenheit
2. Slice carrot into paper-thin shaped coins using a peeler
3. Place slices in a bowl and toss with oil and spices
4. Layout the slices onto a parchment paper-lined baking sheet in a single layer
5. Sprinkle salt
6. Transfer to oven and bake for 8-10 minutes
7. Remove and serve
8. Enjoy!

**Nutritions:** *Calories: 434, Fat: 35g, Carbohydrates: 31g, Protein: 2g*

# 55. HEARTY BRUSSELS AND PISTACHIO

## INGREDIENTS

- 1-pound Brussels sprouts, tough bottom trimmed and halved lengthwise
- 4 shallots, peeled and quartered
- 1 tablespoon extra-virgin olive oil
- Sea salt
- Freshly ground black pepper
- ½ cup roasted pistachios, chopped
- Zest of ½ lemon
- Juice of ½ lemon

## DIRECTIONS

1. Preheat your oven to 400 degrees Fahrenheit
2. Take a baking sheet and line it with aluminum foil
3. Keep it on the side
4. Take a large bowl and add Brussels and shallots and dress them with olive oil
5. Season with salt and pepper and spread veggies onto a sheet
6. Bake for 15 minutes until slightly caramelized
7. Remove the oven and transfer to a serving bowl
8. Toss with lemon zest, lemon juice, and pistachios
9. Serve and enjoy!

**Nutritions:** *Calories: 126, Fat: 7g, Carbohydrates: 14g, Protein: 6g*

# 56. BUFFALO CASHEWS

## INGREDIENTS

- 2 cups raw cashews
- ¾ cup red hot sauce
- 1/3 cup avocado oil
- ½ teaspoon garlic powder
- ¼ teaspoon turmeric

## DIRECTIONS

1. Mix wet ingredients in a bowl and stir in seasoning
2. Add cashews to the bowl and mix
3. Soak cashews in hot sauce mix for 2-4 hours
4. Preheat your oven to 325 degrees Fahrenheit
5. Spread cashews onto a baking sheet
6. Bake for 35-55 minutes, turn every 10-15 minutes
7. Let them cool and serve!

**Nutritions:** *Calories: 268, Fat: 16g, Carbohydrates: 20g, Protein: 14g*

# 57. MORNING PEACH

## INGREDIENTS

- 6 small peaches, cored and cut into wedges
- ¼ cup of coconut sugar
- 2 tablespoons almond butter
- ¼ teaspoon almond extract

## DIRECTIONS

1. Take a small pan and add peaches, sugar, butter and almond extract
2. Toss well
3. Cook over medium-high heat for 5 minutes, divide the mix into bowls and serve
4. Enjoy!

**Nutritions:** *Calories: 198, Fat: 2g, Carbohydrates: 11g, Protein: 8g*

# 58. STICKY MANGO RICE

## INGREDIENTS

- 1/2 cup sugar
- 1 mango, sliced
- 14 ounces coconut milk, canned
- 1/2 cup basmati rice

## DIRECTIONS

1. Cook the rice according to package instructions, add half of the sugar while cooking rice. Make sure to substitute half of the required water with coconut milk
2. Take another skillet and boil remaining coconut milk with sugar, once the mixture is thick add rice and gently stir
3. Add mango slices and serve
4. Enjoy!

**Nutritions:** *Calories: 550, Fat: 30g, Carbohydrates: 70g, Protein: 6g*

# 59. PECAN AND BLUEBERRY CRUMBLE

## INGREDIENTS

- 14 ounces blueberries
- 1 tablespoon lemon juice, fresh
- 1 and ½ teaspoon stevia powder
- 3 tablespoons chia seeds
- 2 cups almond flour, blanched
- ¼ cup pecans, chopped
- 5 tablespoons coconut oil
- 2 tablespoons cinnamon

## DIRECTIONS

1. Take a bowl and mix in blueberries, stevia, chia seeds, and lemon juice and stir
2. Take an iron skillet and place it overheat, add mixture and stir
3. Take a bowl and mix in remaining ingredients, spread mixture over blueberries
4. Preheat your oven to 400 degrees Fahrenheit
5. Transfer baking dish to your oven, bake for 30 minutes
6. Serve and enjoy!

**Nutritions:** *Calories: 380, Fat: 32g, Carbohydrates: 20g, Protein: 10g*

# 60. HEALTHY RICE PUDDING

## INGREDIENTS

- 1 cup of brown rice
- 1 teaspoon vanilla extract
- ½ teaspoon salt
- ½ teaspoon cinnamon
- ¼ teaspoon nutmeg
- 3 egg substitutes
- 3 cups coconut milk, light
- 2 cups brown rice, cooked

## DIRECTIONS

1. Take a bowl and mix in all ingredients, stir well
2. Preheat your oven to 300 degrees Fahrenheit
3. Transfer mixture to a baking dish and transfer dish to the oven
4. Bake for 90 minutes
5. Serve and enjoy!

**Nutritions:** *Calories: 330, Fat: 10g, Carbohydrates: 52g, Protein: 5g*

# 61. OATMEAL COOKIES

## INGREDIENTS

- 1/4 cup applesauce
- 1/2 teaspoon cinnamon
- 1/3 cup raisins
- 1/2 teaspoon vanilla extract, pure
- 1 cup ripe banana, mashed
- 2 cups oatmeal

## DIRECTIONS

1. Preheat your oven to 350 degrees Fahrenheit
2. Take a bowl and mix in everything until you have a gooey mixture
3. Pour batter into ungreased baking sheet drop by drop and flatten them using a tablespoon
4. Transfer to your oven, bake for 15 minutes
5. Serve once ready!

**Nutritions:** *Calories: 80, Fat: 1g, Carbohydrates: 16g, Protein: 2g*

# 62. APPLE SLICES

## INGREDIENTS

- 1 cup of coconut oil
- ¼ cup date paste
- 2 tablespoons ground cinnamon
- 4 granny smith apples, peeled and sliced, cored

## DIRECTIONS

1. Take a large-sized skillet and place it over medium heat
2. Add oil and allow the oil to heat up
3. Stir cinnamon and date paste into the oil
4. Add cut up apples and cook for 5-8 minutes until crispy
5. Serve and enjoy!

**Nutritions:** *Calories: 368, Fat: 23g, Carbohydrates: 44g, Protein: 1g*

# 63. EASY PORTOBELLO MUSHROOMS

## INGREDIENTS

- 12 cherry tomatoes
- 2 ounces scallions
- 4 Portobello mushrooms
- 4 and ¼ ounces of almond butter
- Sunflower seeds and pepper to taste

## DIRECTIONS

1. Take a large skillet and melt almond butter over medium heat
2. Add mushrooms and sauté for 3 minutes
3. Stir in cherry tomatoes and scallions
4. Sauté for 5 minutes
5. Season accordingly
6. Sauté until veggies are tender
7. Enjoy!

**Nutritions:** Calories: 154, Fat: 10g, Carbohydrates: 2g, Protein: 7g

# 64. THE GARBANZO BEAN EXTRAVAGANZA

## INGREDIENTS

- 1 can garbanzo beans, chickpeas
- 1 tablespoon olive oil
- 1 teaspoon sunflower seeds
- 1 teaspoon garlic powder
- ½ teaspoon paprika

## DIRECTIONS

1. Preheat your oven to 375 degrees Fahrenheit
2. Line a baking sheet with silicone baking mat
3. Drain and rinse garbanzo beans, pat garbanzo beans dry and put into a large bowl
4. Toss with olive oil, sunflower seeds, garlic powder, paprika and mix well
5. Spread over a baking sheet
6. Bake for 20 minutes at 375 degrees Fahrenheit
7. Turn chickpeas so they are roasted well
8. Place back in the oven and bake for 25 minutes at 375 degrees Fahrenheit
9. Let them cool and enjoy!

**Nutritions:** *Calories: 395, Fat: 7g, Carbohydrates: 52g, Protein: 35g*

# 65. ROASTED ONIONS AND GREEN BEANS

## INGREDIENTS

- 1 yellow onion, sliced into rings
- ½ teaspoon onion powder
- 2 tablespoons coconut flour
- 1 and 1/3 pounds fresh green beans, trimmed and chopped

## DIRECTIONS

1. Take a large bowl and mix sunflower seeds with onion powder and coconut flour
2. Add onion rings
3. Mix well to coat
4. Spread the rings on the baking sheet, lined with parchment paper
5. Drizzled with some oil
6. Bake for 10 minutes at 400 Fahrenheit
7. Parboil the green beans for 3 to 5 minutes in the boiling water
8. Drain and serve the beans with baked onion rings
9. Eat warm and enjoy!

**Nutritions:** *Calories: 214, Fat: 19.4g, Carbohydrates:3.7g, Protein: 8.3g*

# 66. LEMONY SPROUTS

## INGREDIENTS

- 1-pound Brussels, trimmed and shredded
- 8 tablespoons olive oil
- 1 lemon, juiced and tested
- Salt and pepper to taste
- ¾ cup spicy almond and seed mix

## DIRECTIONS

1. Take a bowl and mix in lemon juice, salt, pepper and olive oil
2. Mix well
3. Stir in shredded Brussels and toss
4. Let it sit for 10 minutes
5. Add nuts and toss
6. Serve and enjoy!

**Nutritions:** *Calories: 382, Fat: 36g, Carbohydrates: 9g, Protein: 7g*

# CHAPTER 12:
# SNACK AND SIDES RECIPES PART 2

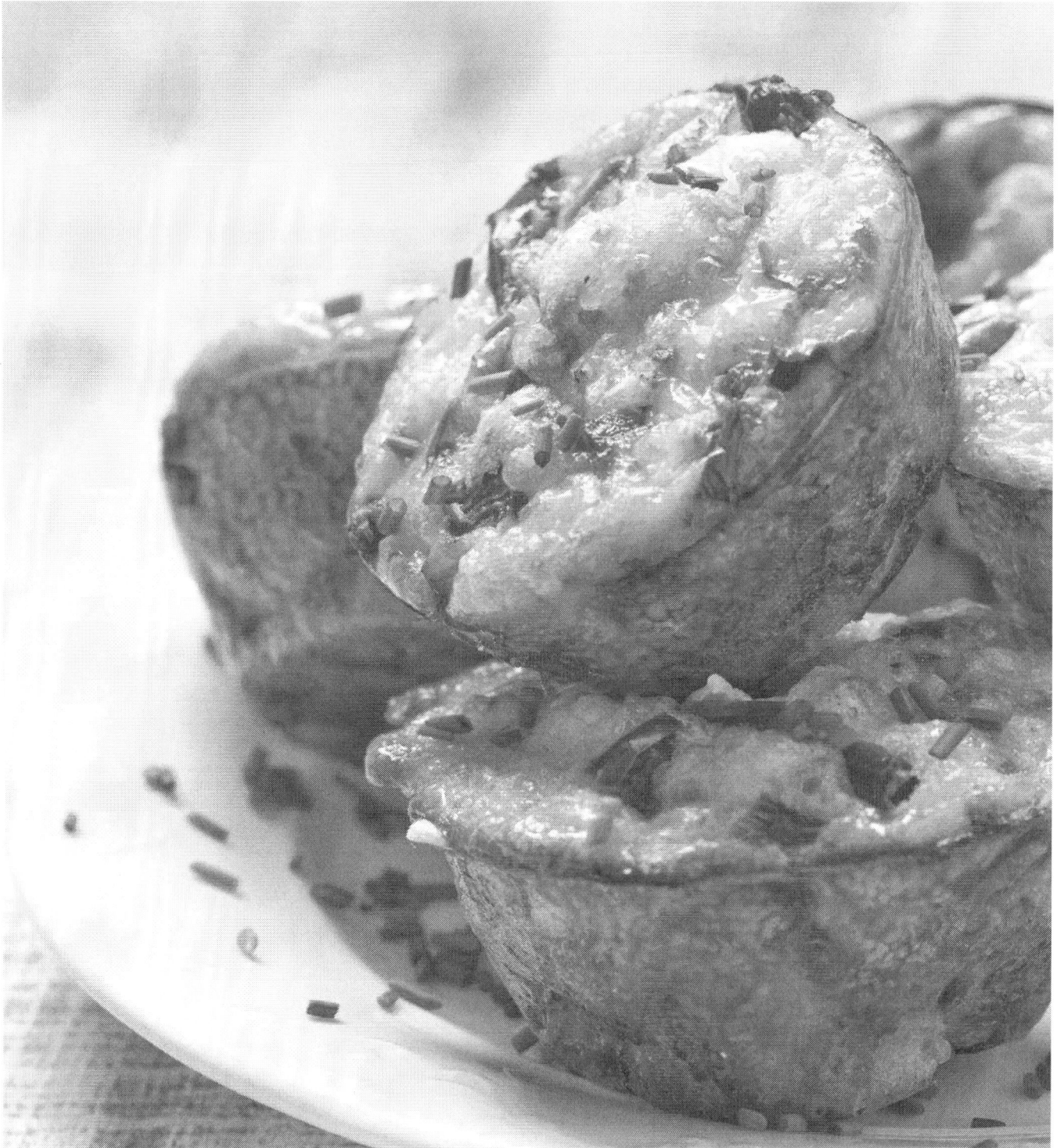

# 67. SAUSAGE ROLLS

## INGREDIENTS

- Whole-wheat bread – 2 slices
- Mixed nuts, halves and pieces - .5 cup
- Onion, small, diced – 1
- Cranberries, dried – 2 tablespoons
- Sea salt – 1.5 teaspoons
- Thyme, fresh, chopped – 1 teaspoon
- Sage, dried – 1 teaspoon
- Fennel seeds - .5 teaspoon
- Paprika, smoked – 1 teaspoon
- Paprika, sweet – 1 teaspoon
- Garlic, minced – 3 cloves
- Black pepper, ground - .25 teaspoon
- Tamari sauce – 1.5 tablespoons
- Sriracha – 1 teaspoon
- Aquafaba egg replacement – 2 tablespoons
- Tofu, firm – 10 ounces
- Vegan puff pastry – 3 prepared sheets

## DIRECTIONS

1. Preheat your large baking oven to a temperature of Fahrenheit three-hundred and seventy-five degrees and prepare a large sheet for baking with either non-stick silicone or kitchen parchment.
2. In a large food processor, pulse together the sliced bread, mixed nuts, cranberries, and herbs until they form a fine meal or crumb.
3. Into the food processor, along with the bread and nut mixture, add the tofu, sea salt, tamari sauce, sriracha, aquafaba, ground black pepper, and both the smoked and sweet paprika. Pulse this mixture until it is well combined, stirring the sides of the container with a spatula as needed. Set this aside.
4. Lay out the three prepared sheets of puff pastry on a cutting board and slice each sheet into four evenly-sized squares so that you end up with twelve squares in all.
5. Divide the tofu sausage mixture between the twelve squares, placing the mixture in the center of each puff pastry piece. Roll the squares up so that the filling is completely contained by the puff pastry.
6. Using a sharp knife cut each of the twelve rolls in half so that you end up with twenty-four smaller sausage rolls. Place all twenty-four sausage rolls on the prepared baking tray with the seam side of the puff pastry facing downward. This will prevent the filling from falling out during the cooking process.
7. Place the sausage rolls in the oven until the puff pastry is golden, about twenty to twenty-five minutes. Serve the rolls alone or with your favorite complimentary chutney.

**Nutritions:** *Calories: 308, Protein 13g, Fat 18g, Total Carbohydrates 25g, Net Carbohydrates 22g*

# 68. ONION RINGS

## INGREDIENTS

- Sweet onions, large – 2
- Soy milk, unsweetened - .66 cup
- Flour - .66 cup
- Nutritional yeast – 1 tablespoon
- Garlic powder – 1 teaspoon
- Paprika, smoked – 1 teaspoon
- Sea salt – 1 teaspoon
- Panko bread crumbs (vegan) – 1 cup

## DIRECTIONS

1. Preheat the oven to a temperature of Fahrenheit three-hundred and fifty degrees before lining a large baking sheet with either non-stick silicone or kitchen parchment.
2. In a medium-sized bowl for the purpose of mixing whisk together the flour, nutritional yeast, garlic powder, smoked paprika, and unsweetened soy milk until there are no clumps remaining. Set this batter aside while you prepare the onions.
3. Peel the large sweet onions and then cut them into rings about one-quarter of an inch thick before carefully separating the rings from each other, avoiding breaking them.
4. Place the panko bread crumbs in a separate bowl for mixing and then begin to coat the onion rings. To do this, you first dip the rings one to two at a time in the batter. After the rings are coated in the batter, you then coat them in the panko bread crumb mixture.
5. Place the battered and coated onion rings on the prepared baking pans and allow them to cook for twenty minutes, flipping them over halfway through the cooking time to ensure they become evenly crispy.
6. Serve the onion rings immediately either on their own or with your favorite dipping sauce.

**Nutritions:** *Calories: 256, Protein 7g Fat 1g, Total Carbohydrates 49g, Net Carbohydrates 46g*

# 69. ALMOND-DATE ENERGY BITES

## INGREDIENTS

- 1 cup dates, pitted
- 1 cup unsweetened shredded coconut
- ¼ cup chia seeds
- ¾ cup ground almonds
- ¼ cup cocoa nibs, or non-dairy chocolate chips

## DIRECTIONS

1. Purée everything in a food processor until crumbly and sticking together, pushing down the sides whenever necessary to keep it blending. If you don't have a food processor, you can mash soft Medjool dates. But if you're using harder baking dates, you'll have to soak them and then try to purée them in a blender.
2. Form the mix into 24 balls and place them on a baking sheet lined with parchment or waxed paper. Put in the fridge to set for about 15 minutes. Use the softest dates you can find. Medjool dates are the best for this purpose. The hard dates you see in the baking aisle of your supermarket are going to take a long time to blend up. If you use those, try soaking them in water for at least an hour before you start, and then draining.

**Nutritions:** *Calories: 152, Total Fat: 11g, Carbs: 13g, Fiber: 5g, Protein: 3g*

# 70. PUMPKIN PIE CUPS (PRESSURE COOKER)

## INGREDIENTS

- 1 cup canned pumpkin purée
- 1 cup nondairy milk
- 6 tablespoons unrefined sugar or pure maple syrup (less if using sweetened milk), plus more for sprinkling
- ¼ cup spelt flour or all-purpose flour
- ½ teaspoon pumpkin pie spice
- Pinch salt

## DIRECTIONS

1. Preparing the ingredients. In a medium bowl, stir together the pumpkin, milk, sugar, flour, pumpkin pie spice, and salt. Pour the mixture into 4 heat-proof ramekins. Sprinkle a bit more sugar on the top of each, if you like. Put a trivet in the bottom of your electric pressure cooker's cooking pot and pour in a cup or two of water. Place the ramekins onto the trivet, stacking them if needed (3 on the bottom, 1 on top).
2. High pressure for 6 minutes. Close and lock the lid and ensure the pressure valve is sealed, then select high pressure and set the time for 6 minutes.
3. Pressure release. Once the cook time is complete, quick release the pressure, being careful not to get your fingers or face near the steam release. Once all the pressure has released, carefully unlock and remove the lid. Let cool for a few minutes before carefully lifting out the ramekins with oven mitts or tongs. Let cool for at least 10 minutes before serving.

**Nutritions:** *Calories: 129, Total Fat: 1g, Protein: 3g, Sodium: 39mg, Fiber: 3g*

# 71. FUDGY BROWNIES (PRESSURE COOKER)

## INGREDIENTS

- 3 ounces dairy-free dark chocolate
- 1 tablespoon coconut oil or vegan margarine
- ½ cup applesauce
- 2 tablespoons unrefined sugar
- ⅓ cup all-purpose flour
- ½ teaspoon baking powder
- Pinch salt

## DIRECTIONS

1. Preparing the ingredients. Put a trivet in your electric pressure cooker's cooking pot and pour in a cup or two of two of water. Select sauté or simmer. In a large heat-proof glass or ceramic bowl, combine the chocolate and coconut oil. Place the bowl over the top of your pressure cooker, as you would a double boiler. Stir occasionally until the chocolate is melted, then turn off the pressure cooker. Stir the applesauce and sugar into the chocolate mixture. Add the flour, baking powder, and salt and stir just until combined. Pour the batter into 3 heat-proof ramekins. Put them in a heat-proof dish and cover with aluminum foil. Using a foil sling or silicone helper handles, lower the dish onto the trivet. (alternately, cover each ramekin with foil and place them directly on the trivet, without the dish.)
2. High pressure for 6 minutes. Close and lock the lid and ensure the pressure valve is sealed, then select high pressure and set the time for 5 minutes.
3. Pressure release. Once the cook time is complete, quick release the pressure, being careful not to get your fingers or face near the steam release. Once all the pressure has released, carefully unlock and remove the lid.
4. Let cool for a few minutes before carefully lifting out the dish, or ramekins, with oven mitts or tongs. Let cool for a few minutes more before serving.
5. Top with fresh raspberries and an extra drizzle of melted chocolate.

**Nutritions:** *Calories: 316, Total Fat: 14g, Protein: 5g, Sodium: 68mg, Fiber: 5g*

# 72. CHOCOLATE PUDDING

## INGREDIENTS

- 1 banana
- 2 to 4 tablespoons nondairy milk
- 2 tablespoons unsweetened cocoa powder
- 2 tablespoons sugar (optional)
- ½ ripe avocado or 1 cup silken tofu (optional)

## DIRECTIONS

1. In a small blender, combine the banana, milk, cocoa powder, sugar (if using), and avocado (if using). Purée until smooth. Alternatively, in a small bowl, mash the banana very well, and stir in the remaining ingredients.

**Nutritions:** *Calories: 244, Protein: 4g, Total Fat: 3g, Saturated fat: 1g, Carbohydrates: 59g, Fiber: 8g*

# 73. AVOCADO PUDDING

## INGREDIENTS

- 2 ripe avocados, peeled, pitted and cut into pieces
- 1 tbsp fresh lime juice
- 14 oz can coconut milk
- 80 drops of liquid stevia
- 2 tsp vanilla extract

## DIRECTIONS

1. Add all ingredients into the blender and blend until smooth.
2. Serve and enjoy.

**Nutritions:** *Calories 317, Fat 30.1 g, Carbohydrates 9.3 g, Sugar 0.4 g, Protein 3.4 g, Cholesterol 0 mg*

# 74. ALMOND BUTTER BROWNIES

## INGREDIENTS

- 1 scoop protein powder
- 2 tbsp cocoa powder
- 1/2 cup almond butter, melted
- 1 cup bananas, overripe

## DIRECTIONS

1. Preheat the oven to 350 f/ 176 c.
2. Spray brownie tray with cooking spray.
3. Add all ingredients into the blender and blend until smooth.
4. Pour batter into the prepared dish and bake in preheated oven for 20 minutes.
5. Serve and enjoy.

**Nutritions:** *Calories 82, Fat 2.1 g, Carbohydrates 11.4 g, Protein 6.9 g, Sugars 5 g, Cholesterol 16 mg*

# 75. RASPBERRY CHIA PUDDING

## INGREDIENTS

- 4 tbsp chia seeds
- 1 cup coconut milk
- 1/2 cup raspberries

## DIRECTIONS

1. Add raspberry and coconut milk in a blender and blend until smooth.
2. Pour mixture into the mason jar.
3. Add chia seeds in a jar and stir well.
4. Close jar tightly with lid and shake well.
5. Place in refrigerator for 3 hours.
6. Serve chilled and enjoy.

**Nutritions:** *Calories 361, Fat 33.4 g, Carbohydrates 13.3 g, Sugar 5.4 g, Protein 6.2 g*

# 76. CHOCOLATE FUDGE

## INGREDIENTS

- 4 oz unsweetened dark chocolate
- 3/4 cup coconut butter
- 15 drops liquid stevia
- 1 tsp vanilla extract

## DIRECTIONS

1. Melt coconut butter and dark chocolate.
2. Add ingredients to the large bowl and combine well.
3. Pour mixture into a silicone loaf pan and place in refrigerator until set.
4. Cut into pieces and serve.

**Nutritions:** *Calories 157, Fat 14.1 g, Carbohydrates 6.1 g, Sugar 1 g, Protein 2.3 g, Cholesterol 0 mg*

# CHAPTER 13:
# VEGETABLES RECIPES

# 77. STEAMED CAULIFLOWER

## INGREDIENTS

- 1 large head cauliflower
- 1 cup water
- ½ teaspoon salt
- 1 teaspoon red pepper flakes (optional)

## DIRECTIONS

1. Remove any leaves from the cauliflower, and cut it into florets.
2. In a large saucepan, bring the water to a boil. Place a steamer basket over the water, and add the florets and salt. Cover and steam for 5 to 7 minutes, until tender. In a large bowl, toss the cauliflower with the red pepper flakes (if using). Transfer the florets to a large airtight container or 6 single-serving containers. Let cool before sealing the lids.

**Nutritions:** *Calories: 35, Fat: 0, Protein: 3g, Carbohydrates: 7g, Fiber: 4g, Sugar: 4g, Sodium: 236mg*

# 78. CAJUN SWEET POTATOES

## INGREDIENTS

- 2 pounds sweet potatoes
- 2 teaspoons extra-virgin olive oil
- ½ teaspoon ground cayenne pepper
- ½ teaspoon smoked paprika
- ½ teaspoon dried oregano
- ½ teaspoon dried thyme
- ½ teaspoon garlic powder
- ½ teaspoon salt (optional)

## DIRECTIONS

1. Preheat the oven to 400°F. Line a baking sheet with parchment paper.
2. Wash the potatoes, pat dry, and cut into ¾-inch cubes. Transfer to a large bowl, and pour the olive oil over the potatoes.
3. In a small bowl, combine the cayenne, paprika, oregano, thyme, and garlic powder. Sprinkle the spices over the potatoes and combine until the potatoes are well coated. Spread the potatoes on the prepared baking sheet in a single layer. Season with the salt (if using). Roast for 30 minutes, stirring the potatoes after 15 minutes.
4. Divide the potatoes evenly among 4 single-serving containers. Let cool completely before sealing.

**Nutritions:** *Calories: 219, Fat: 3g, Protein: 4g, Carbohydrates: 46g, Fiber: 7g, Sugar: 9g, Sodium: 125mg*

# 79. SMOKY COLESLAW

## INGREDIENTS

- 1-pound shredded cabbage
- ⅓ cup vegan mayonnaise
- ¼ cup unseasoned rice vinegar
- 3 tablespoons plain vegan yogurt or plain soymilk
- 1 tablespoon vegan sugar
- ½ teaspoon salt
- ¼ teaspoon freshly ground black pepper
- ¼ teaspoon smoked paprika
- ¼ teaspoon chipotle powder

## DIRECTIONS

1. Put the shredded cabbage in a large bowl. In a medium bowl, whisk the mayonnaise, vinegar, yogurt, sugar, salt, pepper, paprika, and chipotle powder.
2. Pour over the cabbage, and mix with a spoon or spatula and until the cabbage shreds are coated. Divide the coleslaw evenly among 6 single-serving containers. Seal the lids.

**Nutritions:** *Calories: 73, Fat: 4g, Protein: 1g, Carbohydrates: 8g, Fiber: 2g, Sugar: 5g, Sodium: 283mg*

# 80. MEDITERRANEAN HUMMUS PIZZA

## INGREDIENTS

- ½ zucchini, thinly sliced
- ½ red onion, thinly sliced
- 1 cup cherry tomatoes, halved
- 2 to 4 tablespoons pitted and chopped black olives
- Pinch sea salt
- Drizzle olive oil (optional)
- 2 prebaked pizza crusts
- ½ cup Classic Hummus
- 2 to 4 tablespoons Cheesy Sprinkle

## DIRECTIONS

1. Preheat the oven to 400°F. Place the zucchini, onion, cherry tomatoes, and olives in a large bowl, sprinkle them with the sea salt, and toss them a bit. Drizzle with a bit of olive oil (if using), to seal in the flavor and keep them from drying out in the oven.
2. Lay the two crusts out on a large baking sheet. Spread half the hummus on each crust, and top with the veggie mixture and some Cheesy Sprinkle. Pop the pizzas in the oven for 20 to 30 minutes, or until the veggies are soft.

**Nutritions:** *Calories: 500, Total fat: 25g, Carbs: 58g, Fiber: 12g*

# 81. BAKED BRUSSELS SPROUTS

## INGREDIENTS

- 1-pound Brussels sprouts
- 2 teaspoons extra-virgin olive or canola oil
- 4 teaspoons minced garlic (about 4 cloves)
- 1 teaspoon dried oregano
- ½ teaspoon dried rosemary
- ½ teaspoon salt
- ¼ teaspoon freshly ground black pepper
- 1 tablespoon balsamic vinegar

## DIRECTIONS

1. Preheat the oven to 400°F. Line a rimmed baking sheet with parchment paper. Trim and halve the Brussels sprouts. Transfer to a large bowl. Toss with the olive oil, garlic, oregano, rosemary, salt, and pepper to coat well.
2. Transfer to the prepared baking sheet. Bake for 35 to 40 minutes, shaking the pan occasionally to help with even browning, until crisp on the outside and tender on the inside. Remove from the oven and transfer to a large bowl. Stir in the balsamic vinegar, coating well.
3. Divide the Brussels sprouts evenly among 4 single-serving containers. Let cool before sealing the lids.

**Nutritions:** *Calories: 77, Fat: 3g, Protein: 4g, Carbohydrates: 12g, Fiber: 5g, Sugar: 3g, Sodium: 320mg*

# 82. MINTED PEAS

## INGREDIENTS

- 1 tablespoon olive oil
- 4 cups peas, fresh or frozen (not canned)
- ½ teaspoon sea salt
- freshly ground black pepper
- 3 tablespoons chopped fresh mint

## DIRECTIONS

1. In a large sauté pan, heat the olive oil over medium-high heat until hot. Add the peas and cook, about 5 minutes.
2. Remove the pan from heat. Stir in the salt, season with pepper, and stir in the mint.
3. Serve hot.

**Nutritions:** *Calories: 77, Fat: 3g, Protein: 4g, Carbohydrates: 12g, Fiber: 5g, Sugar: 3g, Sodium: 320mg*

# 83. BASIC BAKED POTATOES

## INGREDIENTS

- 5 medium Russet potatoes or a variety of potatoes, washed and patted dry
- 1 to 2 tablespoons extra-virgin olive oil
- ¼ teaspoon salt
- ¼ teaspoon freshly ground black pepper

## DIRECTIONS

1. Preheat the oven to 400°F. Pierce each potato several times with a fork or a knife. Brush the olive oil over the potatoes, then rub each with a pinch of the salt and a pinch of the pepper.
2. Place the potatoes on a baking sheet and bake for 50 to 60 minutes, until tender. Place the potatoes on a baking rack and cool completely. Transfer to an airtight container or 5 single-serving containers. Let cool before sealing the lids.

**Nutritions:** *Calories: 171, Fat: 3g, Protein: 4g, Carbohydrates: 34g, Fiber: 5g, Sugar: 3g, Sodium: 129mg*

# 84. GLAZED CURRIED CARROTS

## INGREDIENTS

- 1-pound carrots, peeled and thinly sliced
- 2 tablespoons olive oil
- 2 tablespoons curry powder
- 2 tablespoons pure maple syrup
- juice of ½ lemon
- sea salt
- freshly ground black pepper

## DIRECTIONS

1. Place the carrots in a large pot and cover with water. Cook on medium-high heat until tender, about 10 minutes. Drain the carrots and return them to the pan over medium-low heat.
2. Stir in the olive oil, curry powder, maple syrup, and lemon juice. Cook, stirring constantly, until the liquid reduces, about 5 minutes. Season with salt and pepper and serve immediately.

**Nutritions:** *Calories: 171, Fat: 3g, Protein: 4g, Carbohydrates: 34g, Fiber: 5g, Sugar: 3g, Sodium: 129mg*

# 85. MISO SPAGHETTI SQUASH

## INGREDIENTS

- 1 (3-pound) spaghetti squash
- 1 tablespoon hot water
- 1 tablespoon unseasoned rice vinegar
- 1 tablespoon white miso

## DIRECTIONS

1. Preheat the oven to 400°F. Line a rimmed baking sheet with parchment paper. Halve the squash lengthwise and place, cut-side down, on the prepared baking sheet.
2. Bake for 35 to 40 minutes, until tender. Cool until the squash is easy to handle. With a fork, scrape out the flesh, which will be stringy, like spaghetti. Transfer to a large bowl. In a small bowl, combine the hot water, vinegar, and miso with a whisk or fork. Pour over the squash. Gently toss with tongs to coat the squash. Divide the squash evenly among 4 single-serving containers. Let cool before sealing the lids.

**Nutritions:** *Calories: 117, Fat: 2g, Protein: 3g, Carbohydrates: 25g, Fiber: 0g, Sugar: 0g, Sodium: 218mg*

# 86. GARLIC AND HERB NOODLES

## INGREDIENTS

- 1 teaspoon extra-virgin olive oil or 2 tablespoons vegetable broth
- 1 teaspoon minced garlic (about 1 clove)
- 4 medium zucchinis, spiral
- ½ teaspoon dried basil
- ½ teaspoon dried oregano
- ¼ to ½ teaspoon red pepper flakes, to taste
- ¼ teaspoon salt (optional)
- ¼ teaspoon freshly ground black pepper

## DIRECTIONS

1. In a large skillet over medium-high heat, heat the olive oil.
2. Add the garlic, zucchini, basil, oregano, red pepper flakes, salt (if using), and black pepper. Sauté for 1 to 2 minutes, until barely tender. Divide the noodles evenly among 4 storage containers. Let cool before sealing the lids.

**Nutritions:** *Calories: 44, Fat: 2g, Protein: 3g, Carbohydrates: 7g, Fiber: 2g, Sugar: 3g, Sodium: 20mg*

# 87. THAI ROASTED BROCCOLI

## INGREDIENTS

- 1 head broccoli, cut into florets
- 2 tablespoons olive oil
- 1 tablespoon soy sauce or gluten-free tamari

## DIRECTIONS

1. Preheat the oven to 425°F. Line a baking sheet with parchment paper. In a large bowl, combine the broccoli, oil, and soy sauce. Toss well to combine.
2. Spread the broccoli on the prepared baking sheet. Roast for 10 minutes.
3. Toss the broccoli with a spatula and roast for an additional 5 minutes, or until the edges of the florets begin to brown.

**Nutritions:** *Calories: 44, Fat: 2g, Protein: 3g, Carbohydrates: 7g, Fiber: 2g, Sugar: 3g, Sodium: 20mg*

# 88. COCONUT CURRY NOODLE

## INGREDIENTS

- ½ tablespoon oil
- 3 garlic cloves, minced
- 2 tablespoons lemongrass, minced
- 1 tablespoon fresh ginger, grated
- 2 tablespoons red curry paste
- 1 (14 oz) can coconut milk
- 1 tablespoon brown sugar
- 2 tablespoons soy sauce
- 2 tablespoons fresh lime juice
- 1 tablespoon hot chili paste
- 12 oz linguine
- 2 cups broccoli florets
- 1 cup carrots, shredded
- 1 cup edamame, shelled
- 1 red bell pepper, sliced

## DIRECTIONS

1. Fill a suitably-sized pot with salted water and boil it on high heat.
2. Add pasta to the boiling water and cook until it is al dente then rinse under cold water.
3. Now place a medium-sized saucepan over medium heat and add oil.
4. Stir in ginger, garlic, and lemongrass, then sauté for 30 seconds.
5. Add coconut milk, soy sauce, curry paste, brown sugar, chili paste, and lime juice.
6. Stir this curry mixture for 10 minutes, or until it thickens.
7. Toss in carrots, broccoli, edamame, bell pepper, and cooked pasta.
8. Mix well, then serve warm.

**Nutritions:** *Calories: 44, Fat: 2g, Protein: 3g, Carbohydrates: 7g, Fiber: 2g, Sugar: 3g, Sodium: 20mg*

# 89. COLLARD GREEN PASTA

## INGREDIENTS

- 2 tablespoons olive oil
- 4 garlic cloves, minced
- 8 oz whole wheat pasta
- ½ cup panko bread crumbs
- 1 tablespoon nutritional yeast
- 1 teaspoon red pepper flakes
- 1 large bunch collard greens
- 1 large lemon, zest and juiced

## DIRECTIONS

1. Fill a suitable pot with salted water and boil it on high heat.
2. Add pasta to the boiling water and cook until it is al dente, then rinse under cold water.
3. Reserve ½ cup of the cooking liquid from the pasta.
4. Place a non-stick pan over medium heat and add 1 tablespoon olive oil.
5. Stir in half of the garlic, then sauté for 30 seconds.
6. Add breadcrumbs and sauté for approximately 5 minutes.
7. Toss in red pepper flakes and nutritional yeast then mix well.
8. Transfer the breadcrumbs mixture to a plate and clean the pan.
9. Add the remaining tablespoon oil to the nonstick pan.
10. Stir in the garlic clove, salt, black pepper, and chard leaves.
11. Cook for 5 minutes until the leaves are wilted.
12. Add pasta along with the reserved pasta liquid.
13. Mix well, then add garlic crumbs, lemon juice, and zest.
14. Toss well, then serve warm.

**Nutritions:** *Calories: 45, Fat: 2.5g, Protein: 4g, Carbohydrates: 9g, Fiber: 4g, Sugar: 3g, Sodium: 20mg*

# CHAPTER 14:
# VEGETABLES RECIPES PART 2

# 90. JALAPENO RICE NOODLES

## INGREDIENTS

- ¼ cup soy sauce
- 1 tablespoon brown sugar
- 2 teaspoons sriracha
- 3 tablespoons lime juice
- 8 oz rice noodles
- 3 teaspoons toasted sesame oil
- 1 package extra-firm tofu, pressed
- 1 onion, sliced
- 2 cups green cabbage, shredded
- 1 small jalapeno, minced
- 1 red bell pepper, sliced
- 1 yellow bell pepper, sliced
- 3 garlic cloves, minced
- 3 scallions, sliced
- 1 cup Thai basil leaves, roughly chopped
- Lime wedges for serving

## DIRECTIONS

1. Fill a suitably-sized pot with salted water and boil it on high heat.
2. Add pasta to the boiling water and cook until it is al dente, then rinse under cold water.
3. Put lime juice, soy sauce, sriracha, and brown sugar in a bowl then mix well.
4. Place a large wok over medium heat then add 1 teaspoon sesame oil.
5. Toss in tofu and stir for 5 minutes until golden-brown.
6. Transfer the golden-brown tofu to a plate and add 2 teaspoons oil to the wok.
7. Stir in scallions, garlic, peppers, cabbage, and onion.
8. Sauté for 2 minutes, then add cooked noodles and prepared sauce.
9. Cook for 2 minutes, then garnish with lime wedges and basil leaves.
10. Serve fresh.

**Nutritions:** *Calories: 45, Fat: 2.5g, Protein: 4g, Carbohydrates: 9g, Fiber: 4g, Sugar: 3g, Sodium: 20mg*

# 91. RAINBOW SOBA NOODLES

## INGREDIENTS

- 8 oz tofu, pressed and crumbled
- 1 teaspoon olive oil
- ½ teaspoon red pepper flakes
- 10 oz package buckwheat soba noodles, cooked
- 1 package broccoli slaw
- 2 cups cabbage, shredded
- ¼ cup very red onion, thinly sliced
- Peanut Sauce
- ¼ cup peanut butter
- ¾ cup hot water
- 2 tablespoons apple cider vinegar
- 1 tablespoon maple syrup
- 1–2 garlic cloves, minced
- 1 lime, zest, and juice
- Salt and crushed red pepper flakes, to taste
- Cilantro, for garnish
- Crushed peanuts, for garnish

## DIRECTIONS

1. Crumble tofu on a baking sheet and toss in 1 teaspoon oil and 1 teaspoon red pepper flakes.
2. Bake the tofu for 20 minutes at 400°F in a preheated oven.
3. Meanwhile, whisk peanut butter with hot water, garlic cloves, maple syrup, cider vinegar, lime zest, salt, lime juice, and pepper flakes in a large bowl.
4. Toss in cooked noodles, broccoli slaw, cabbages, and onion.
5. Mix well, then stir in tofu, cilantro, and peanuts.
6. Enjoy.

**Nutritions:** *Calories: 45, Fat: 2.5g, Protein: 4g, Carbohydrates: 9g, Fiber: 4g, Sugar: 3g, Sodium: 20mg*

# 92. SPICY PAD THAI PASTA

## INGREDIENTS

**Spicy Tofu**
- 1 lb extra-firm tofu, sliced
- 1 tablespoon peanut butter
- 3 tablespoons soy sauce
- 2 tablespoons Sriracha
- 2 tablespoons rice vinegar
- 2 teaspoons sesame oil
- 2 teaspoons ginger, grated

**Pad Thai**
- 8 oz brown rice noodles
- 2 teaspoons coconut oil
- 1 red pepper, sliced
- ½ white onion, sliced
- 2 carrots, sliced
- 1 Thai chili, chopped
- ½ cup peanuts, chopped
- ½ cup cilantro, chopped

**Spicy Pad Thai Sauce**
- 3 tablespoons soy sauce
- 3 tablespoons fresh lime juice
- 1 tablespoon Sriracha
- 3 tablespoons brown sugar
- 3 tablespoons vegetable broth
- 1 teaspoon garlic-chili paste
- 2 garlic cloves, minced

## DIRECTIONS

1. Fill a suitably-sized pot with water and soak rice noodles in it.
2. Press the tofu to squeeze excess liquid out of it.
3. Place a non-stick pan over medium-high heat and add tofu.
4. Sear the tofu for 2-3 minutes per side until brown.
5. Whisk all the ingredients for tofu crumbles in a large bowl.
6. Stir in tofu and mix well.
7. Separately mix the pad Thai sauce in a bowl and add to the tofu.
8. Place a wok over medium heat and add 1 teaspoon oil.
9. Toss in chili, carrots, onion, and red pepper, then sauté for 3 minutes.
10. Transfer the veggies to the tofu bowl.
11. Add more oil to the same pan and stir in drained noodles, then stir cook for 1 minute.
12. Transfer the noodles to the tofu and toss it all well.
13. Add cilantro and peanuts.
14. Serve fresh.

**Nutritions:** *Calories: 45, Fat: 2.5g, Protein: 4g, Carbohydrates: 9g, Fiber: 4g, Sugar: 3g, Sodium: 20mg*

# 93. LINGUINE WITH WINE SAUCE

## INGREDIENTS

- 1 tablespoon olive oil
- 5 garlic cloves, minced
- 16 oz shiitake, chopped
- ¼ teaspoon salt
- ¼ teaspoon ground pepper
- 1 pinch red pepper flakes
- ½ cup dry white wine
- 12 oz linguine
- 2 teaspoons vegan butter
- ¼ cup Italian parsley, finely chopped

## DIRECTIONS

1. Fill a suitably-sized pot with salted water and bring it to a boil on high heat.
2. Add pasta to the boiling water then cook until it is al dente, then rinse under cold water.
3. Place a non-stick skillet over medium-high heat then add olive oil.
4. Stir in garlic and sauté for 1 minute.
5. Stir in mushrooms and cook for 10 minutes.
6. Add salt, red pepper flakes, and black pepper for seasoning.
7. Toss in the cooked pasta and mix well.
8. Garnish with parsley and butter.
9. Enjoy.

**Nutritions:** *Calories: 40, Fat: 2.0g, Protein: 5g, Carbohydrates: 7g, Fiber: 4g, Sugar: 3g, Sodium: 18mg*

# 94. CHEESY MACARONI WITH BROCCOLI

## INGREDIENTS

- 1/3 cup melted coconut oil
- ¼ cup nutritional yeast
- 1 tablespoon tomato paste
- 1 tablespoon dried mustard
- 2 garlic cloves, minced
- 1 ½ teaspoons salt
- ½ teaspoon ground turmeric
- 4 ½ cups almond milk
- 3 cups cauliflower florets, chopped
- 1 cup raw cashews, chopped
- 1 lb shell pasta
- 1 tablespoon white vinegar
- 3 cups broccoli florets

## DIRECTIONS

1. Place a suitably-sized saucepan over medium heat and add coconut oil.
2. Stir in mustard, yeast, garlic, salt, tomato paste, and turmeric.
3. Cook for 1 minute then add almond milk, cashews, and cauliflower florets.
4. Continue cooking for 20 minutes on a simmer.
5. Transfer the cauliflower mixture to a blender jug then blend until smooth.
6. Stir in vinegar and blend until creamy.
7. Fill a suitably-sized pot with salted water and bring it to a boil on high heat.
8. Add pasta to the boiling water.
9. Place a steamer basket over the boiling water and add broccoli to the basket.
10. Cook until the pasta is al dente. Drain and rinse the pasta and transfer the broccoli to a bowl.
11. Add the cooked pasta to the cauliflower-cashews sauce.
12. Toss in broccoli florets, salt, and black pepper.
13. Mix well then serve.

**Nutritions:** *Calories: 40, Fat: 2.0g, Protein: 5g, Carbohydrates: 7g, Fiber: 4g, Sugar: 3g, Sodium: 18mg*

# 95. SOBA NOODLES WITH TOFU

## INGREDIENTS

### Marinated Tofu
- 2 tablespoons olive oil
- 8 oz firm tofu, pressed and drained
- ¼ cup cilantro, finely chopped
- ¼ cup mint, finely chopped
- 1-inch fresh ginger, grated

### Soba Noodles
- 8 oz soba noodles
- ¾ cup edamame
- 2 cucumbers, peeled and julienned
- 1 large carrot, peeled and julienned
- 2 tablespoons black sesame seeds
- 2 tablespoons white sesame seeds
- 2 scallions, chopped

### Ginger-Soy Sauce
- 2 tablespoons fresh lime juice
- 2 tablespoons soy sauce
- 1 tablespoon brown sugar
- 1 tablespoon fresh ginger, grated
- 2 tablespoons sesame oil
- ½ tablespoon garlic chili sauce

## DIRECTIONS

1. Blend herbs, ginger, salt, black pepper, and olive oil in a blender.
2. Add the spice mixture to the tofu and toss it well to coat.
3. Allow the tofu to marinate for 30 minutes at room temperature.
4. Fill a suitably-sized pot with salted water and bring it to a boil on high heat.
5. Add pasta to the boiling water then cook until it is al dente, then rinse under cold water.
6. Place a large wok over medium heat and add marinated tofu.
7. Sauté for 5–8 minutes until golden-brown, then transfer to a large bowl.
8. Add veggies to the same wok and stir until veggies are soft.
9. Transfer the veggies to the tofu and add cooked noodles.
10. Toss well, then serve warm.
11. Enjoy.

**Nutritions:** *Calories: 30, Fat: 3.5.0g, Protein: 6g, Carbohydrates: 6g, Fiber: 4g, Sugar: 5g, Sodium: 18mg*

# 96. PLANT BASED KETO LO MEIN

## INGREDIENTS

- 2 tablespoons carrots, shredded
- 1 package kelp noodles, soaked in water
- 1 cup broccoli, frozen

**For the Sauce**
- 1 tablespoon sesame oil
- 2 tablespoons tamari
- ½ teaspoon ground ginger
- ¼ teaspoon Sriracha
- ½ teaspoon garlic powder

## DIRECTIONS

1. Put the broccoli in a saucepan on medium low heat and add the sauce ingredients.
2. Cook for about 5 minutes and add the noodles after draining water.
3. Allow to simmer about 10 minutes, occasionally stirring to avoid burning.
4. When the noodles have softened, mix everything well and dish out to serve.

**Nutritions:** *Calories: 30, Fat: 3.5.0g, Protein: 6g, Carbohydrates: 6g, Fiber: 4g*

# 97. VEGETARIAN CHOW MEIN

## INGREDIENTS

- ½ large onion, chopped
- ½ small leek, chopped
- ½ tablespoon ginger paste
- ½ tablespoon Worcester sauce
- ½ tablespoon Oriental seasoning
- ½ teaspoon parsley
- Salt and black pepper, to taste
- ½ pound noodles
- 2 large carrots, diced
- 2 celery sticks, chopped
- 1 tablespoon olive oil
- ½ teaspoon garlic paste
- 1½ tablespoons soy sauce
- 1 tablespoon Chinese five spice
- ½ teaspoon coriander
- 2 cups water

## DIRECTIONS

1. Put olive oil, ginger, garlic paste, and onion in a pot on medium heat and sauté for about 5 minutes.
2. Stir in all the vegetables and cook for about5 minutes.
3. Add rest of the ingredients and combine well.
4. Secure the lid and cook on medium heat for about 20 minutes, stirring occasionally.
5. Open the lid and dish out to serve hot.

**Nutritions:** *Calories: 30, Fat: 3.5.0g, Protein: 6g, Carbohydrates: 6g, Fiber: 4g, Sugar: 5g, Sodium: 18mg*

# 98. VEGGIE NOODLES

## INGREDIENTS

- 2 tablespoons vegetable oil
- 4 spring onions, divided
- 1 cup snap pea
- 2 tablespoons brown sugar
- 9 oz. dried rice noodles, cooked
- 5 garlic cloves, minced
- 2 carrots, cut into small sticks
- 3 tablespoons soy sauce

## DIRECTIONS

1. Heat vegetable oil in a skillet over medium heat and add garlic and 3 spring onions.
2. Cook for about 3 minutes and add the carrots, peas, brown sugar and soy sauce.
3. Add rice noodles and cook for about 2 minutes.
4. Season with salt and black pepper and top with remaining spring onion to serve.

**Nutritions:** *Calories: 25, Fat: 2.0g, Protein: 5.2g, Carbohydrates: 5.3g, Fiber: 4g, Sodium: 18mg*

# 99. MINUTES VEGETARIAN PASTA

## INGREDIENTS

- 3 shallots, chopped
- ¼ teaspoon red pepper flakes
- ¼ cup vegan parmesan cheese
- 2 tablespoons olive oil
- 2 garlic cloves, minced
- 8-ounces spinach leaves
- 8-ounces linguine pasta
- 1 pinch salt
- 1 pinch black pepper

## DIRECTIONS

1. Boil salted water in a large pot and add pasta.
2. Cook for about 6 minutes and drain the pasta in a colander.
3. Heat olive oil over medium heat in a large skillet and add the shallots.
4. Cook for about 5 minutes until soft and caramelized and stir in the spinach, garlic, red pepper flakes, salt and black pepper.
5. Cook for about 5 minutes and add pasta and 2 ladles of pasta water.
6. Stir in the parmesan cheese and dish out in a bowl to serve.

**Nutritions:** *Calories: 25, Fat: 2.0g, Protein: 5.2g, Carbohydrates: 5.3g, Fiber: 4g, Sodium: 18mg*

# 100. ASIAN VEGGIE NOODLES

## INGREDIENTS

- ½ cup peas
- 1 teaspoon rice vinegar
- 3 carrots, chopped
- 1 small packet vermicelli
- 3 tablespoons sesame oil
- 1 red pepper, chopped in small cubes
- 1 can baby corn
- 1 clove garlic, chopped
- 2 tablespoons soy sauce
- 1 teaspoon ginger powder
- ½ teaspoon curry powder
- Salt and black pepper, to taste

## DIRECTIONS

1. Take a bowl and add ginger powder, vinegar, soy sauce, curry powder, and a pinch of salt to it.
2. Cook the noodles according to the instructions and drain them.
3. Heat the sesame oil and cook vegetables in it for 10 minutes on medium heat.
4. Add noodles to it and cook for 3 more minutes.
5. Remove from heat and serve to enjoy.

**Nutritions:** *Calories: 25, Fat: 2.0g, Protein: 5.2g, Carbohydrates: 5.3g, Fiber: 4g, Sodium: 18mg*

# CHAPTER 15:
# SALADS RECIPES

# 101. BROCCOLI SALAD

## INGREDIENTS

- 2 tablespoons sherry vinegar
- ¼ cup olive oil
- 2 teaspoons fresh thyme, chopped
- 1 teaspoon Dijon mustard
- 1 teaspoon honey
- Salt to taste
- 8 cups broccoli florets, steamed or roasted
- 2 red onions, sliced thinly
- ½ cup Parmesan cheese, shaved
- ¼ cup pecans, toasted and chopped

## DIRECTIONS

1. Mix the sherry vinegar, olive oil, thyme, mustard, honey and salt in a bowl.
2. In a serving bowl, combine the broccoli florets and onions.
3. Drizzle the dressing on top.
4. Sprinkle with the pecans and Parmesan cheese before serving.

**Nutritions:** *Calories 199, Fat 17.4 g, Saturated fat 2.9 g, Carbohydrates 7.5 g, Fiber 2.8 g, Protein 5.2 g*

# 102. POTATO CARROT SALAD

## INGREDIENTS

- Water
- 6 potatoes, sliced into cubes
- 3 carrots, sliced into cubes
- 1 tablespoon milk
- 1 tablespoon Dijon mustard
- ¼ cup mayonnaise
- Pepper to taste
- 2 teaspoons fresh thyme, chopped
- 1 stalk celery, chopped
- 2 scallions, chopped
- 1 slice turkey bacon, cooked crispy and crumbled

## DIRECTIONS

1. Fill your pot with water.
2. Place it over medium high heat.
3. Boil the potatoes and carrots for 10 minutes or until tender.
4. Drain and let cool.
5. In a bowl, mix the milk mustard, mayo, pepper and thyme.
6. Stir in the potatoes, carrots and celery.
7. Coat evenly with the sauce.
8. Cover and refrigerate for 4 hours.
9. Top with the scallions and turkey bacon bits before serving.

**Nutritions:** *Calories 106, Fat 5.3 g, Saturated fat 1 g, Carbohydrates 12.6 g, Fiber 1.8g, Protein 2 g*

# 103. PEA SALAD

## INGREDIENTS

- 1 cup chickpeas, rinsed and drained
- 1 ½ cups peas, divided
- Salt to taste
- 3 tablespoons olive oil
- ½ cup buttermilk
- Pepper to taste
- 8 cups pea greens
- 3 carrots, shaved
- 1 cup snow peas, trimmed

## DIRECTIONS

1. Add the chickpeas and half of the peas to your food processor.
2. Season with the salt.
3. Pulse until smooth. Set aside.
4. In a bowl, toss the remaining peas in oil, milk, salt and pepper.
5. Transfer the mixture to your food processor.
6. Process until pureed.
7. Transfer this mixture to a bowl.
8. Arrange the pea greens in a serving plate.
9. Top with the shaved carrots and snow peas.
10. Stir in the pea and milk dressing.
11. Serve with the reserved chickpea hummus.

**Nutritions:** *Calories 214, Fat 8.6 g, Saturated fat 1.5 g, Carbohydrates 27.3 g, Fiber 8.4 g, Protein 8 g*

# 104. SNAP PEA SALAD

## INGREDIENTS

- 2 tablespoons mayonnaise
- ¾ teaspoon celery seed
- ¼ cup cider vinegar
- 1 teaspoon yellow mustard
- 1 tablespoon sugar
- Salt and pepper to taste
- 4 oz. radishes, sliced thinly
- 12 oz. sugar snap peas, sliced thinly

## DIRECTIONS

1. In a bowl, combine the mayonnaise, celery seeds, vinegar, mustard, sugar, salt and pepper.
2. Stir in the radishes and snap peas.
3. Refrigerate for 30 minutes.

**Nutritions:** *Calories 69, Fat 3.7 g, Saturated fat 0.6 g, Carbohydrates 7.1 g, Fiber 1.8 g, Protein 2 g*

# 105. CUCUMBER TOMATO CHOPPED SALAD

## INGREDIENTS

- ½ cup light mayonnaise
- 1 tablespoon lemon juice
- 1 tablespoon fresh dill, chopped
- 1 tablespoon chives, chopped
- ½ cup feta cheese, crumbled
- Salt and pepper to taste
- 1 red onion, chopped
- 1 cucumber, diced
- 1 radish, diced
- 3 tomatoes, diced
- Chives, chopped

## DIRECTIONS

1. Combine the mayo, lemon juice, fresh dill, chives, feta cheese, salt and pepper in a bowl.
2. Mix well.
3. Stir in the onion, cucumber, radish and tomatoes.
4. Coat evenly.
5. Garnish with the chopped chives.

**Nutritions:** *Calories 187, Fat 16.7 g, Saturated fat 4.1 g, Carbohydrates 6.7 g, Fiber 2 g, Protein 3.3 g*

# 106. ZUCCHINI PASTA SALAD

## INGREDIENTS

- 5 tablespoons olive oil
- 2 teaspoons Dijon mustard
- 3 tablespoons red-wine vinegar
- 1 clove garlic, grated
- 2 tablespoons fresh oregano, chopped
- 1 shallot, chopped
- ¼ teaspoon red pepper flakes
- 16 oz. zucchini noodles
- ¼ cup Kalamata olives, pitted
- 3 cups cherry tomatoes, sliced in half
- ¾ cup Parmesan cheese, shaved

## DIRECTIONS

1. Mix the olive oil, Dijon mustard, red-wine vinegar, garlic, oregano, shallot and red pepper flakes in a bowl.
2. Stir in the zucchini noodles.
3. Sprinkle on top the olives, tomatoes and Parmesan cheese.

**Nutritions:** *Calories 299, Fat 24.7 g, Saturated fat 5.1 g, Carbohydrates 11.6 g, Fiber 2.8 g, Protein 7 g*

# 107. EGG AVOCADO SALAD

## INGREDIENTS

- 1 avocado
- 6 hard-boiled eggs, peeled and chopped
- 1 tablespoon mayonnaise
- 2 tablespoons freshly squeezed lemon juice
- ¼ cup celery, chopped
- 2 tablespoons chives, chopped
- Salt and pepper to taste

## DIRECTIONS

1. Add the avocado to a large bowl.
2. Mash the avocado using a fork.
3. Stir in the egg and mash the eggs.
4. Add the mayo, lemon juice, celery, chives, salt and pepper.
5. Chill in the refrigerator for at least 30 minutes before serving.

**Nutritions:** *Calories 224, Fat 18 g, Saturated fat 3.9 g, Carbohydrates 6.1 g, Fiber 3.6 g, Protein 10.6 g*

# 108. PEPPER TOMATO SALAD

## INGREDIENTS

- 2 tablespoons balsamic vinegar
- 2 tablespoons olive oil
- ½ teaspoon Dijon mustard
- 2 teaspoons fresh basil leaves, chopped
- 1 tablespoon fresh chives, chopped
- 1 teaspoon sugar
- Pepper to taste
- 2 cups yellow bell peppers, sliced into rings
- 1 cups orange bell pepper, sliced into rings
- 4 tomatoes, sliced into rounds
- ¼ cup blue cheese, crumbled

## DIRECTIONS

1. Mix the vinegar, olive oil, mustard, basil, chives, sugar and pepper in a bowl.
2. Arrange the tomatoes and pepper rings in a serving plate.
3. Sprinkle the crumbled blue cheese on top.
4. Drizzle with the dressing.
5. Chill in the refrigerator for 1 hour before serving.

**Nutritions:** *Calories 116, Fat 7 g, Saturated fat 2 g, Carbohydrates 11 g, Fiber 2 g, Protein 3 g*

# 109. PENNE WITH VEGGIES

## INGREDIENTS

- 2 teaspoons olive oil
- 2 cloves garlic, crushed and minced
- ½ cup shallots, chopped
- 2 tablespoons dry white wine
- 1 cup Brussels sprouts, trimmed and chopped
- 6 cups bok choy, chopped
- 6 cups cooked penne pasta
- 1 tablespoons vegetable oil spread
- Salt and pepper to taste
- 2 teaspoons dried Italian seasoning
- 3 tablespoons Parmesan cheese, grated

## DIRECTIONS

1. Pour the oil into a pan over medium heat.
2. Cook the garlic and shallots for 3 minutes.
3. Pour in the wine.
4. Scrape the browned bits using a wooden spoon.
5. Stir in the Brussels sprouts.
6. Cook for 3 minutes.
7. Stir in the bok choy and cook for 2 to 3 minutes.
8. Toss the pasta in the veggies.
9. Add the vegetable oil into the mix.
10. Season with the salt, pepper and Italian seasoning.
11. Sprinkle the Parmesan cheese on top.

**Nutritions:** *Calories 127, Fat 4 g, Saturated fat 1 g, Carbohydrates 17 g, Fiber 3 g, Protein 6 g*

# 110. MARINATED VEGGIE SALAD

## INGREDIENTS

- 1 zucchini, sliced
- 4 tomatoes, sliced into wedges
- ¼ cup red onion, sliced thinly
- 1 green bell pepper, sliced
- 2 tablespoons fresh parsley, chopped
- 2 tablespoons red-wine vinegar
- 2 tablespoons olive oil
- 1 clove garlic, minced
- 1 teaspoon dried basil
- 2 tablespoons water
- Pine nuts, toasted and chopped

## DIRECTIONS

1. In a bowl, combine the zucchini, tomatoes, red onion, green bell pepper and parsley.
2. Pour the vinegar and oil into a glass jar with lid.
3. Add the garlic, basil and water.
4. Seal the jar and shake well to combine.
5. Pour the dressing into the vegetable mixture.
6. Cover the bowl.
7. Marinate in the refrigerator for 4 hours.
8. Garnish with the pine nuts before serving.

**Nutritions:** *Calories 65, Fat 4.7 g, Saturated fat 0.7 g, Carbohydrates 5.3 g, Fiber 1.2 g, Protein 0.9 g*

# 111. ARUGULA SALAD

## INGREDIENTS

- 6 cups fresh arugula leaves
- 2 cups radicchio, chopped
- ¼ cup low-fat balsamic vinaigrette
- ¼ cup pine nuts, toasted and chopped

## DIRECTIONS

1. Arrange the arugula leaves in a serving bowl.
2. Sprinkle the radicchio on top.
3. Drizzle with the vinaigrette.
4. Sprinkle the pine nuts on top.

**Nutritions:** *Calories 85, Fat 6.6 g, Saturated fat 0.5 g, Carbohydrates 5.1 g, Fiber 1 g, Protein 2.2 g*

# 112. MEDITERRANEAN SALAD

## INGREDIENTS

- 2 teaspoons balsamic vinegar
- 1 tablespoon basil pesto
- 1 cup lettuce
- ¼ cup broccoli florets, chopped
- ½ cup zucchini, chopped
- ¼ cup tomato, chopped
- ¼ cup yellow bell pepper, chopped
- 2 tablespoons feta cheese, crumbled

## DIRECTIONS

1. Arrange the lettuce on a serving platter.
2. Top with the broccoli, zucchini, tomato and bell pepper.
3. In a bowl, mix the vinegar and pesto.
4. Drizzle the dressing on top.
5. Sprinkle the feta cheese and serve.

**Nutritions:** *Calories 100, Fat 6 g, Saturated fat 1 g, Carbohydrates 7 g, Protein 4 g*

# 113. POTATO TUNA SALAD

## INGREDIENTS

- Water
- 3 potatoes, peeled and sliced into cubes
- ½ cup plain yogurt
- ½ cup mayonnaise
- 1 clove garlic, crushed and minced
- 1 tablespoon almond milk
- 1 tablespoon fresh dill, chopped
- ½ teaspoon lemon zest
- Salt to taste
- 1 cup cucumber, chopped
- ¼ cup scallions, chopped
- ¼ cup radishes, chopped
- 9 oz. canned tuna flakes
- 2 hard-boiled eggs, chopped
- 6 cups lettuce, chopped

## DIRECTIONS

1. Fill your pot with water.
2. Add the potatoes and boil.
3. Cook for 10 minutes or until slightly tender.
4. Drain and let cool.
5. In a bowl, mix the yogurt, mayo, garlic, almond milk, fresh dill, lemon zest and salt.
6. Stir in the potatoes, tuna flakes and eggs.
7. Mix well.
8. Chill in the refrigerator for 4 hours.
9. Stir in the shredded lettuce before serving.

**Nutritions:** *Calories 243, Fat 9.9 g, Saturated fat 2 g, Carbohydrates 22.2 g, Fiber 4.6 g, Protein 17.5 g*

# 114. SHRIMP VEGGIE PASTA SALAD

## INGREDIENTS

- 1 lb. shrimp, peeled and deveined
- 8 oz. asparagus, sliced
- Salt and pepper to taste
- 12 oz. farfalle, penne or macaroni pasta, cooked
- 2 tablespoons parsley, chopped
- ½ cup shallots, sliced thinly
- ¼ cup Parmesan cheese, grated
- 2 tablespoons freshly squeezed lemon juice
- ½ cup mayonnaise
- 2 teaspoons garlic, minced
- 1 teaspoon Worcestershire sauce
- 1 teaspoon Dijon mustard
- 1 lemon, sliced into wedges

## DIRECTIONS

1. Preheat your oven to 400 degrees F.
2. Arrange the shrimp and asparagus in a baking pan.
3. Season with the salt and pepper.
4. Roast in the oven for 10 minutes.
5. Let cool. Transfer to a bowl.
6. Stir in the cooked pasta, parsley and shallots.
7. Sprinkle the Parmesan cheese on top.
8. In another bowl, combine the lemon juice, mayonnaise, garlic, Worcestershire sauce and Dijon mustard.
9. Add this mixture to the pasta salad.
10. Toss to coat evenly.
11. Refrigerate for at least 30 minutes before serving.
12. Garnish with the lemon wedges.

**Nutritions:** *Calories 429, Fat 17.1 g, Saturated fat 2.8 g, Carbohydrates 45.6 g, Fiber 7.2 g, Protein 25 g*

# 115. SAUTÉED CABBAGE

## INGREDIENTS

- ¼ cup butter
- 1 onion, sliced thinly
- 1 head cabbage, sliced into wedges
- Salt and pepper to taste
- Crumbled crispy bacon bits

## DIRECTIONS

1. Add the butter to a pan over medium high heat.
2. Cook the onion for 1 minute, stirring frequently.
3. Season with the salt and pepper.
4. Add the cabbage and cook while stirring for 12 minutes.
5. Sprinkle with the crispy bacon bits.

**Nutritions:** *Calories 77, Fat 5.9 g, Saturated fat 3.6 g, Carbohydrates 6.1 g, Fiber 2.4 g, Protein 1.3 g*

# CHAPTER 16:
# SALADS RECIPES PART 2

# 116. JICAMA AND SPINACH SALAD RECIPE

## INGREDIENTS

### Salad
- 10 oz baby spinach, washed and dried
- Grape or cherry tomatoes, cut in half
- 1 jicama, washed, peeled, and cut in strips
- Green or Kalamata olives, chopped
- 8 tsp walnuts, chopped
- 1 tsp raw or roasted sunflower seeds
- Maple Mustard Dressing

### Dressing
- 1 heaping tbsp Dijon mustard
- Dash cayenne pepper
- 2 tbsp maple syrup
- 2 garlic cloves, minced
- 1 to 2 tbsp water
- ¼ tsp sea salt

## DIRECTIONS

**For the salad:**
1. Divide the baby spinach onto 4 salad plates. Top each serving with ¼ of the jicama, ¼ of the chopped olives, and 4 tomatoes. Sprinkle 1 tsp of the sunflower seeds and 2 tsp of the walnuts.

**For the dressing:**
2. In a small mixing bowl, whisk all the ingredients together until emulsified. Check the taste and add more maple syrup for sweetness.
3. Drizzle 1½ tbsp of the dressing over each salad and serve.

**Nutritions:** *Calories: 196, Fat: 2 g, Protein: 7 g, Carbs: 28 g, Fiber: 12g*

# 117. HIGH-PROTEIN SALAD

## INGREDIENTS

**Salad**
- 1 15-oz can green kidney beans
- 2 4 tbsp capers
- 3 4 handfuls arugula
- 4 15-oz can lentils

**Dressing**
- 5 1 tbsp caper brine
- 6 1 tbsp tamari
- 7 1 tbsp balsamic vinegar
- 8 2 tbsp peanut butter
- 9 2 tbsp hot sauce
- 10 1 tbsp tahini

## DIRECTIONS

1. For the dressing:
2. In a bowl, whisk together all the ingredients until they come together to form a smooth dressing.
3. For the salad:
4. Mix the beans, arugula, capers, and lentils. Top with the dressing and serve.

**Nutritions:** *Calories: 205, Fat: 2 g, Protein: 13 g, Carbs: 31 g, Fiber: 17g*

# 118. VEGAN WRAP WITH APPLES AND SPICY HUMMUS

## INGREDIENTS

- 1 tortilla
- 6-7 tbsp Spicy Hummus (mix it with a few tbsp of salsa)
- A few leaves of fresh spinach or romaine lettuce
- 1 tsp fresh lemon juice
- 1½ cups broccoli slaw
- ½ apple, sliced thin
- 4 tsp dairy-free plain unsweetened yogurt
- Salt and pepper

## DIRECTIONS

1. Mix the yogurt and the lemon juice with the broccoli slaw. Add the salt and a dash of pepper for taste. Mix well and set aside.
2. Lay the tortilla flat.
3. Spread the spicy hummus over the tortilla.
4. Lay the lettuce down on the hummus.
5. On one half, pile the broccoli slaw on the lettuce.
6. Place the apple slices on the slaw.
7. Fold the sides of the tortilla up, starting with the end that has the apple and the slaw. Roll tightly.
8. Cut it in half and serve.

**Nutritions:** *Calories: 205, Fat: 2 g, Protein: 12 g, Carbs: 32 g, Fiber: 9g*

# 119. RICE AND VEGGIE BOWL

## INGREDIENTS

- 2 tbsp coconut oil
- 1 tsp ground cumin
- 1 tsp ground turmeric
- 1 tsp chili powder
- 1 red bell pepper, chopped
- 1 tsp tomato paste
- 1 bunch of broccolis, cut into bite-sized florets with short stems
- 1 tsp salt, to taste
- 1 large red onion, sliced
- 2 garlic cloves, minced
- 1 head of cauliflower, cut into bite-sized florets
- 2 cups cooked rice (or other cooked grain)
- Freshly ground black pepper to taste

## DIRECTIONS

1. In a large pan or skillet, heat the coconut oil over medium-high heat.
2. When the oil is hot, stir in the turmeric, cumin, chili powder, salt, and tomato paste.
3. Cook the content for 1 minute. Stir repeatedly until the spices are fragrant.
4. Add the garlic and onion. Sauté for 2 to 3 minutes until the onions are softened.
5. Add the broccoli, cauliflower, and bell pepper. Cover. Cook for 3 to 4 minutes and stir occasionally.
6. Add the cooked rice. Stir so it will combine well with the vegetables. Cook for 2 to 3 minutes. Stir until the rice is warmed through.
7. Check the seasoning and adjust to taste if desired.
8. Lower the heat and cook on low for 2 to 3 more minutes so the flavors will meld.
9. Serve with freshly ground black pepper.

**Nutritions:** *Calories: 260, Fat: 9 g, Protein: 9 g, Carbs: 36 g, Fiber: 5g*

# 120. SQUASH BLACK BEAN BOWL

## INGREDIENTS

- 1 large spaghetti squash, halved, seeded
- ⅓ cup water (or 2 tbsp olive oil, rubbed on inside of squash)
- Black bean filling
- 1 15-oz can of black beans, drained and rinsed
- 1 cup fire-roasted corn (or frozen sweet corn)
- 1 cup thinly sliced red cabbage
- 3 tbsp chopped green onion, green and white parts
- ¼ cup chopped fresh cilantro
- ½ lime, juiced or to taste
- Pepper and salt, to taste

**Avocado mash**
- 1 ripe avocado, mashed
- ½ lime, juiced or to taste
- ¼ tsp cumin
- Pepper and pinch of sea salt

## DIRECTIONS

1. Preheat the oven to 400°F.
2. Cut the squash in half and scoop out the seeds with a spoon, like a pumpkin.
3. Fill the roasting pan with ⅓ cup of water. Lay the squash, cut side down, in the pan. Bake for 25 to 30 minutes until soft and tender.
4. While this is baking, mix all the ingredients for the black bean filling in a medium-sized bowl.
5. In a small bowl, mash the avocado and mix in the ingredients for the avocado mash.
6. Remove the squash from the oven and let it cool for 5 minutes. Scrape the squash with a fork so that it looks like spaghetti noodles. Then, fill it with black bean filling and top with avocado mash.
7. Serve and enjoy.

**Nutritions:** *Calories: 85, Fat: 0.5 g, Protein: 4 g, Carbs: 6 g, Fiber: 4g*

# 121. RED BEANS BOWL

## INGREDIENTS

- 3½ cups water, divided
- 1 tsp red pepper flakes
- 3 stalks celery, diced
- 1 green pepper, chopped
- ½ yellow onion, diced
- 2 small cans kidney beans, drained and rinsed
- 1 cup brown rice
- 3 garlic cloves, minced
- 1 bay leaf
- 1 tsp sage
- ½ tsp oregano
- ½ tsp cayenne
- Optional for heat: 1-2 jalapenos, diced

## DIRECTIONS

1. Add 1 cup of rice and 2 cups of water to a pot. Bring the contents to a boil, turn down the heat, and cover to simmer until the water is absorbed.
2. Once the rice is cooked, on low-medium heat, put all the remaining ingredients in a large saucepan and cover for 20 to 30 minutes. Stir occasionally until the onions are cooked and the 1 cup of water has boiled off.
3. Serve and enjoy.

**Nutritions:** *Calories: 221, Fat: 1 g, Protein: 11 g, Carbs: 25 g, Fiber: 4g*

# 122. ZUCCHINI WITH WHITE BEANS AND TOMATO

## INGREDIENTS

- 4 oz dried spaghetti
- 6 garlic cloves, peeled and sliced
- 2 medium zucchinis, spiral
- ¼ cup extra virgin olive oil
- 1 cup halved cherry tomatoes
- Pinch of red pepper flakes
- 1 (15-oz) can cannellini beans, drained and rinsed
- ¼ cup fresh basil or Italian parsley

## DIRECTIONS

1. Bring a pot of salted water to a boil and add spaghetti. Cook according to the package directions. Drain and add to a large serving bowl with the zucchini noodles. The heat from the pasta will cook the noodles.
2. Sauté the sliced garlic with the pepper flakes in olive oil in the same pot over low heat.
3. Cook until the garlic is tender. This should take about 5 minutes. Be careful to not burn the garlic.
4. Add the tomatoes, beans, and both kinds of noodles back to the pot. Toss to coat with olive oil and garlic. Heat until the beans and zucchini noodles are heated. Stir in parsley or basil.
5. Season accordingly with sea salt. Serve with parmesan if you choose.

**Nutritions:** *Calories: 301, Fat: 15 g, Protein: 11 g, Carbs: 34 g, Fiber: 7g*

# 123. KALE AND QUINOA

## INGREDIENTS

- 1 medium sweet potato, diced
- 2 tsp coconut oil
- ¼ cup cooked quinoa
- 2 cups kale
- 4 brown rice paper wraps
- Pepper and salt, to taste

**Dressing**
- 3 tbsp tahini
- ½ tsp ground ginger
- 3 tsp lemon juice
- 1½ tsp wheat-free tamari
- 1 small garlic clove, grated
- Water as needed
- 1 tsp miso paste

## DIRECTIONS

1. Preheat the oven to 400°F.
2. Toss the sweet potatoes with the oil. Season with salt and pepper.
3. Place on the baking sheet. Roast for 20 to 25 minutes until it starts to brown.
4. As the potato roasts, toss the quinoa and kale with 1 tbsp of dressing. Massage until the kale softens slightly. Set it aside.
5. In a large bowl of warm water, dip 1 rice paper at a time. Once the papers are slightly soft, put them on a clean surface.
6. Lay the quinoa-kale mixture on the center of the paper. Top it with some potato. Fold in both sides, like a burrito, then fold the closest edge over the filling. Tightly, roll away from you. Repeat the process with the rice papers.
7. To serve, slice in half and dip in the dressing.

**Nutritions:** *Calories: 408, Fat: 17 g, Protein: 13 g, Carbs: 53 g, Fiber: 4g*

# 124. GRILLED ASPARAGUS

## INGREDIENTS

- 2 slices sourdough bread
- 10 Asparagus spears
- 4 tbsp chickpea flour
- 2 tbsp nutritional yeast (optional)
- 1 tsp black salt (optional)
- ½ tsp garlic powder
- Pepper and salt, to taste

## DIRECTIONS

1. Preheat the grill. Mix the nutritional yeast, chickpea flour, garlic powder, and black salt (if you are using).
2. Stir in 1 tbsp of water until you get a thick and pourable consistency.
3. Spread the mixture on the bread slices. Arrange the asparagus spears on top.
4. Grill for about 8 minutes until the chickpea mixture firms up and the asparagus is properly cooked.
5. Serve on its own or with mushrooms or grilled tomatoes.
6. Enjoy!

**Nutritions:** *Calories: 270, Fat: 3 g, Protein: 14 g, Carbs: 52 g*

# 125. QUINOA BROCCOLI

## INGREDIENTS

- 4 heaping cups broccoli florets (2 cups steamed, chopped)
- 1 tsp miso paste
- 3 flax eggs
- 2 tbsp flaxseed meal
- 8 tbsp water
- ½ cup nutritional yeast
- 1 tsp garlic powder
- 2 tbsp quinoa flour
- 2 tbsp hummus

## DIRECTIONS

1. Add the broccoli to a steamer basket. Steam about 5 minutes until tender.
2. As the broccoli steams, whisk the flaxseed meal and water together and set aside.
3. Allow the broccoli to cool for about 5 or 10 minutes. Transfer the contents to a cutting board, then chop. Transfer to a large bowl.
4. Add the remaining ingredients to the mixing bowl, including the flax eggs. Starting with 1 tbsp of hummus, stir together until a dough is formed. If the contents are dry, add more hummus.
5. Line a baking sheet with parchment paper. Form the dough into small balls. Let it chill for 30 minutes in the fridge.
6. When you are ready to bake, preheat the oven to 400°F. Bake this for 18 to 20 minutes and flip at about 10 minutes.
7. Allow the tots to cool for 10 or 15 minutes. Transfer to a plate. Serve and enjoy.

**Nutritions:** *Calories: 45, Fat: 4 g, Protein: 13 g, Carbs: 2 g, Fiber: 3g*

# 126. POLENTA WITH PEARS AND CRANBERRIES

## INGREDIENTS

- 2 pears, cored, diced
- 1 tsp ground cinnamon
- ¼ cup brown rice syrup
- 1 cup dried or fresh cranberries
- 1 batch basic polenta

## DIRECTIONS

1. In a medium saucepan, heat the brown rice syrup and add the cranberries, cinnamon, and pears. Cook. Stir continuously until the pears are tender. This should take about 10 minutes.
2. Divide the polenta in 4 individual bowls. Top with the pear compote and serve.
3. Enjoy!

**Nutritions:** *Calories: 200, Fat: 13 g, Protein: 4 g, Carbs: 17 g, Fiber: 3g*

# CHAPTER 17:
# BEANS AND GRAINS RECIPES

# 127. BLACK BEAN & SWEET POTATO HASH

## INGREDIENTS

- 1 cup onion, chopped
- 2 garlic cloves, minced
- 2 cups sweet potatoes, chopped and peeled
- 2 tsp hot chili powder
- ⅓ cup vegetable broth
- 1 cup cooked black beans
- ¼ cup chopped scallions
- Chopped cilantro, for garnish
- Hot sauce (optional)

## DIRECTIONS

1. In a nonstick skillet, place the onion and sauté over medium heat. Stir occasionally for 2 to 3 minutes. Add the garlic and stir.
2. Add the chili pepper and sweet potatoes. Stir to coat the vegetables with chili powder.
3. Add the broth and stir. Cook the contents for 12 minutes and stir occasionally until the potatoes are well-cooked.
4. Add some liquid. This will keep the vegetables from sticking to the pan. Add the scallions, black beans, and salt. Cook for 1 or 2 minutes until the beans are well-heated.
5. Add the hot sauce, if you are using it. Stir. Check the taste and adjust accordingly with the seasoning.
6. Top it with cilantro.

**Nutritions:** *Calories: 270, Fat: 7 g, Protein: 13 g, Carbs: 35 g, Fiber: 7g*

# 128. SWEET AND SALTY PINEAPPLE FRIED RICE

## INGREDIENTS

**Rice**

- 2 tbsp coconut oil
- 2/3 cup frozen green peas, thawed
- ½ cup sunflower seeds (raw)
- Red pepper (one large), diced
- 3 cups canned or fresh pineapple chunks
- 2 garlic cloves, minced
- 1 tbsp ginger, minced
- 2 cups long-grain brown rice, cooked
- Green onions (one bunch)

**Sauce**

- 1 cup pineapple juice
- 4 tbsp tamari
- 1 tsp sesame oil
- Lime juice (half a lime)
- Chili sauce to taste (sriracha is a good option)

## DIRECTIONS

1. On medium heat in a large pan, toast the sunflower seeds for about 2 minutes. Set aside when the content is lightly browned.
2. On medium heat using the same pan, heat the coconut oil. Add the red pepper, pineapple chunks, and 2/3 of the green onion. Stir for about 5 minutes.
3. Now add the garlic and ginger. Stir so the tastes can meld.
4. Keep the heat on high. Add the cold rice and cook for 5 minutes until it is toasty.
5. Fold in the green peas as well as the toasted seeds
6. With the pan still on medium heat, pour in the tamari, sesame oil, and pineapple juice. Stir.
7. Season as required with the chili sauce.
8. For a better taste, add more lime juice and salt as required.

**Nutritions:** *Calories: 180, Fat: 11 g, Protein: 18 g, Carbs: 38 g, Fiber: 12g*

# 129. RICE & VEGGIE BOWL

## INGREDIENTS

- 2 tbsp coconut oil
- 1 tsp ground cumin
- 1 tsp ground turmeric
- 1 tsp chili powder
- 1 red bell pepper, chopped
- 1 tsp tomato paste
- 1 bunch of broccolis, cut into bite-sized florets with short stems
- 1 tsp salt, to taste
- 1 large red onion, sliced
- 2 garlic cloves, minced
- 1 head of cauliflower, cut into bite-sized florets
- 2 cups cooked rice (or other cooked grain)
- Freshly ground black pepper to taste

## DIRECTIONS

1. In a large pan or skillet, heat the coconut oil over medium-high heat.
2. When the oil is hot, stir in the turmeric, cumin, chili powder, salt, and tomato paste.
3. Cook the content for 1 minute. Stir repeatedly until the spices are fragrant.
4. Add the garlic and onion. Sauté for 2 to 3 minutes until the onions are softened.
5. Add the broccoli, cauliflower, and bell pepper. Cover. Cook for 3 to 4 minutes and stir occasionally.
6. Add the cooked rice. Stir so it will combine well with the vegetables. Cook for 2 to 3 minutes. Stir until the rice is warmed through.
7. Check the seasoning and adjust to taste if desired.
8. Lower the heat and cook on low for 2 to 3 more minutes so the flavors will meld.
9. Serve with freshly ground black pepper.

**Nutritions:** *Calories: 260, Fat: 9 g, Protein: 9 g, Carbs: 36 g, Fiber: 5g*

# 130. RED BEANS AND RICE

## INGREDIENTS

- 3½ cups water, divided
- 1 tsp red pepper flakes
- 3 stalks celery, diced
- 1 green pepper, chopped
- ½ yellow onion, diced
- 2 small cans kidney beans, drained and rinsed
- 1 cup brown rice
- 3 garlic cloves, minced
- 1 bay leaf
- 1 tsp sage
- ½ tsp oregano
- ½ tsp cayenne
- Optional for heat: 1-2 jalapenos, diced

## DIRECTIONS

1. Add 1 cup of rice and 2 cups of water to a pot. Bring the contents to a boil, turn down the heat, and cover to simmer until the water is absorbed.
2. Once the rice is cooked, on low-medium heat, put all the remaining ingredients in a large saucepan and cover for 20 to 30 minutes. Stir occasionally until the onions are cooked and the 1 cup of water has boiled off.

**Nutritions:** *Calories: 221, Fat: 1 g, Protein: 11 g, Carbs: 25 g, Fiber: 4g*

# 131. RAW NOODLES WITH AVOCADO 'N NUTS

## INGREDIENTS

- 1 zucchini
- 1½ c. basil
- 1/3 c. water
- 5 tbsps. pine nuts
- 2 tbsps. lemon juice
- 1 avocado, peeled, pitted, sliced
- Optional: 2 tbsps. olive oil
- 6 yellow cherry tomatoes, halved
- Optional: 6 red cherry tomatoes, halved
- Sea salt and black pepper

## DIRECTIONS

1. Add the basil, water, nuts, lemon juice, avocado slices, optional olive oil (if desired), salt, and pepper to a blender.
2. Blend the ingredients into a smooth mixture. Season with more pepper and salt and blend again.
3. Divide the sauce and the zucchini noodles between two medium-sized bowls for serving, and combine in each.
4. Top the mixtures with the halved yellow cherry tomatoes, and the optional red cherry tomatoes (if desired);

**Nutritions:** *Calories 317, Carbs 7.4 g, Fats 28.1 g, Protein 7.2 g*

# 132. RICE & BEAN BURRITOS

## INGREDIENTS

- 32 oz. fat-free refried beans
- 6 tortillas
- 2 c. cooked rice
- ½ c. salsa
- 1 tbsp. olive oil
- 1 bunch green onions, chopped
- 2 bell peppers, chopped
- Guacamole

## DIRECTIONS

1. Preheat the oven to 375°F.
2. Dump the refried beans into a saucepan and place over medium heat to warm.
3. Heat the tortillas and lay them out on a flat surface.
4. Spoon the beans in a long mound that runs across the tortilla, just a little off from center.
5. Spoon some rice and salsa over the beans; add the green pepper and onions to taste, along with any other finely chopped vegetables you like.
6. Fold over the shortest edge of the plain tortilla and roll it up, folding in the sides as you go.
7. Place each burrito, seam side down, on a nonstick-sprayed baking sheet.
8. Brush with olive oil and bake for 15 minutes.

**Nutritions:** *Calories 290, Carbs 49 g, Fats 6 g, Protein 9 g*

# 133. BARBECUED GREENS & GRITS

## INGREDIENTS

- 14 oz. tempeh, sliced
- 3 c. vegetable broth
- 3 c. collard greens, chopped
- ½ c. BBQ sauce
- 1 c. gluten-free grits
- ¼ c. white onion, diced
- 2 tbsps. olive oil
- 2 garlic cloves, minced
- 1 tsp. salt

## DIRECTIONS

1. Preheat the oven to 400°F.
2. Mix tempeh slices with the BBQ sauce in a shallow baking dish. Set aside and let marinate for up to 3 hours.
3. Heat 1 tablespoon of olive oil in a frying pan over medium heat, then add the garlic and sauté until fragrant.
4. Add the collard greens and ½ teaspoon of salt and cook until the collards are wilted and dark. Set the pan from heat and set aside.
5. Cover the tempeh and BBQ sauce mixture with aluminum foil. In your oven, set the baking dish in place and bake the ingredients for 15 minutes. Uncover and continue to bake for another 10 minutes until the tempeh is browned and crispy.
6. While the tempeh cooks heat the remaining tablespoon of olive oil in the previously used frying pan over medium heat.
7. Cook the onions until brown and fragrant, around 10 minutes.
8. Pour in the vegetable broth and bring it to a boil; then turn the heat down to low.
9. Slowly whisk the grits into the simmering broth. Add the remaining ½ teaspoon of salt before covering the pan with a lid.
10. Let the ingredients simmer for about 8 minutes until the grits are soft and creamy.
11. Serve the tempeh and collard greens on top of a bowl of grits and enjoy, or store for later!

**Nutritions:** *Calories 374, Fat 19.1g, Carbs 31.1g, Protein 23.7g*

# 134. CHICKPEA AND SPINACH CUTLETS

## INGREDIENTS

- 1 Red Bell Pepper
- 19 oz. Chickpeas, Rinsed & Drained
- 1 c. ground Almonds
- 2 tsps. Dijon Mustard
- 1 tsp. Oregano
- ½ tsp. Sage
- 1 c. Spinach, Fresh
- 1½ c. Rolled Oats
- 1 Clove Garlic, Pressed
- ½ Lemon, Juiced
- 2 tsps. Maple Syrup, Pure

## DIRECTIONS

1. Get out a baking sheet. Line it with parchment paper.
2. Cut your red pepper in half and then take the seeds out. Place it on your baking sheet, and roast in the oven while you prepare your other ingredients.
3. Process your chickpeas, almonds, mustard, and maple syrup together in a food processor.
4. Add in your lemon juice, oregano, sage, garlic, and spinach, processing again. Make sure it's combined, but don't puree it.
5. Once your red bell pepper is softened, which should roughly take ten minutes, add this to the processor as well. Add in your oats, mixing well.
6. Form twelve patties, cooking in the oven for a half hour. They should be browned.

**Nutritions:** *Calories: 200, Protein: 8 g, Fat: 11g, Carbs: 21 g*

# 135. FLAVORFUL REFRIED BEANS

## INGREDIENTS

- 3 c. rinsed pinto beans
- 1 seeded jalapeno pepper, chopped
- 1 sliced white onion, peeled
- 2 tbsps. minced garlic
- 5 tsps. salt
- 2 tsps. ground black pepper
- ¼ tsps. ground cumin
- 9 c. water

## DIRECTIONS

1. Using a 6-quarts slow cooker, place all the ingredients and stir until it mixes properly.
2. Cover the top, plug in the slow cooker, adjust the cooking time to 6 hours, let it cook on high heat setting, and add more water if the beans get too dry.
3. When beans are done, drain and reserve the liquid.
4. Use a potato masher to mash the beans and pour in the reserved cooking liquid until it reaches your desired mixture.

**Nutritions:** *Calories: 105, Carbs: 36g, Protein: 13g, Fats:1g*

# 136. SMOKY RED BEANS AND RICE

## INGREDIENTS

- 30 oz. cooked red beans
- 1 c. brown rice, uncooked
- 1 c. green pepper, chopped
- 1 c. chopped celery
- 1 c. white onion, chopped
- 1 ½ tsps. minced garlic
- ½ tsp. salt
- ¼ tsp. cayenne pepper
- 1 tsp. smoked paprika
- 2 tsps. dried thyme
- 1 bay leaf
- 2 1/3 c. vegetable broth

## DIRECTIONS

1. Using a 6-quarts slow cooker, place all the ingredients except for the rice, salt, and cayenne pepper.
2. Stir until it mixes properly and then cover the top.
3. Plug in the slow cooker; adjust the cooking time to 4 hours and let it steam on a low heat setting.
4. Then pour in and stir the rice, salt, cayenne pepper and continue cooking for an additional 2 hours at a high heat setting.

**Nutritions:** *Calories:425 Cal, Carbs:62g, Protein:27g, Fats:22g.*

# 137. SAVORY SPANISH RICE

## INGREDIENTS

- 1 c. long grain rice, uncooked
- ½ c. green bell pepper, chopped
- 14 oz. diced tomatoes
- ½ c. chopped white onion
- 1 tsp. minced garlic
- ½ tsp. salt
- 1 tsp. red chili powder
- 1 tsp. ground cumin
- 4 oz. tomato puree
- 8 fl. oz. water

## DIRECTIONS

1. Grease a 6-quarts slow cooker with a non-stick cooking spray and add all the ingredients into it.
2. Stir properly and cover the top.
3. Plug in the slow cooker; adjust the cooking time to 5 hours and let cook on high or until the rice absorbs all the liquid.

**Nutritions:** *Calories: 210 Cal, Carbs: 11g, Protein: 12g, Fats: 10g.*

# CHAPTER 18:
# BEANS AND GRAINS RECIPES PART 2

# 138. DELIGHTFUL COCONUT VEGETARIAN CURRY

## INGREDIENTS

- 5 potatoes, peeled and cubed
- ¼ c. curry powder
- 2 tbsps. flour
- 1 tbsp. chili powder
- ½ tsp. red pepper flakes
- ½ tsp. cayenne pepper
- 1 green bell pepper, chopped
- 1 red bell pepper, chopped
- 2 tbsps. onion soup mix
- 14 oz. coconut cream, unsweetened
- 3 c. vegetable broth
- 2 carrots, peeled and sliced
- 1 c. green peas
- ¼ c. chopped cilantro

## DIRECTIONS

1. Take a 6-quarts slow cooker, grease it with a non-stick cooking spray and place the potatoes pieces in the bottom.
2. Set in the rest of the ingredients except for peas, cilantro, and carrots.
3. Stir properly and cover the top.
4. Plug in the slow cooker; adjust the cooking time to 4 hours and let it cook on the low heat setting or until it cooks thoroughly.
5. When the cooking time is over, add the carrots to the curry and continue cooking for 30 minutes.
6. Stir in the peas to cook for 30 more minutes or until the peas get tender.
7. Garnish it with cilantro and serve.

**Nutritions:** *Calories: 369 Cal, Carbs: 39g, Protein: 7g, Fats: 23g*

# 139. COMFORTING CHICKPEA TAGINE

## INGREDIENTS

- 14 oz. cooked chickpeas
- 12 dried apricots
- 1 red bell pepper, cored and sliced
- 1 cored butternut squash, peeled and chopped
- 2 stemmed zucchinis, chopped
- 1 white onion, peeled and chopped
- 1 tsp. minced garlic
- 1 tsp. ground ginger
- 1 ½ tsps. salt
- 1 tsp. ground black pepper
- 1 tsp. ground cumin
- 2 tsps. paprika
- 1 tsp. harissa paste
- 2 tsps. honey
- 2 tbsps. olive oil
- 1 lb. passata
- ¼ c. chopped coriander

## DIRECTIONS

1. Take a 6-quarts slow cooker, grease it with a non-stick cooking spray and place the chickpeas, apricots, bell pepper, butternut squash, zucchini, and onion into it.
2. Sprinkle it with salt, black pepper, and set it aside until it is called for.
3. Place a large non-stick skillet pan over an average temperature of heat; add the oil, garlic, cumin, and paprika.
4. Stir properly and cook for 1 minutes or until it starts producing fragrance.
5. Then pour in the harissa paste, honey, passata, and boil the mixture.
6. When the mixture is done boiling, pour this mixture over the vegetables in the slow cooker and cover it with the lid.
7. Plug in the slow cooker; adjust the cooking time to 4 hours and let it cook on the high heat setting or until the vegetables gets tender.
8. When done, add the seasoning, garnish it with the coriander, and serve right away.

**Nutritions:** *Calories: 237, Carbs: 45g, Protein :9g, Fats: 2g*

# 140. BLACK BEAN STUFFED SWEET POTATOES

## INGREDIENTS

- 4 sweet potatoes
- 15 oz. cooked black beans
- ½ tsp. ground black pepper
- ½ red onion, peeled, diced
- ½ tsp. sea salt
- ¼ tsp. onion powder
- ¼ tsp. garlic powder
- ¼ tsp. red chili powder
- ¼ tsp. cumin
- 1 tsp. lime juice
- 1 ½ tbsps. olive oil
- ½ c. cashew cream sauce

## DIRECTIONS

1. Spread sweet potatoes on a baking tray greased with foil and bake for 65 minutes at 350 degrees f until tender.
2. Meanwhile, prepare the sauce, and for this, whisk together the cream sauce, black pepper, and lime juice until combined, set aside until required.
3. When 10 minutes of the baking time of potatoes are left, heat a skillet pan with oil. Add in onion to cook until golden for 5 minutes.
4. Then stir in spice, cook for another 3 minutes, stir in bean until combined and cook for 5 minutes until hot.
5. Let roasted sweet potatoes cool for 10 minutes, then cut them open, mash the flesh and top with bean mixture, cilantro and avocado, and then drizzle with cream sauce.
6. Serve straight away.

**Nutritions:** *Calories: 387, Fat: 16.1 g, Carbs: 53 g, Protein: 10.4 g*

# 141. BLACK BEAN AND QUINOA SALAD

## INGREDIENTS

- 15 oz. cooked black beans
- 1 chopped red bell pepper, cored
- 1 c. quinoa, cooked
- 1 cored green bell pepper, chopped
- ½ c. vegan feta cheese, crumbled

## DIRECTIONS

1. In a bowl, set in all ingredients, except for cheese, and stir until incorporated.
2. Top the salad with cheese and serve straight away.

**Nutritions:** *Calories: 64, Fat: 1 g, Carbs: 8 g, Protein: 3 g*

# 142. COCONUT CHICKPEA CURRY

## INGREDIENTS

- 2 tsps. coconut flour
- 16 oz. cooked chickpeas
- 14 oz. tomatoes, diced
- 1 red onion, sliced
- 1 ½ tsps. minced garlic
- ½ tsp. sea salt
- 1 tsp. curry powder
- 1/3 tsp. ground black pepper
- 1 ½ tbsps. garam masala
- ¼ tsp. cumin
- 1 lime, juiced
- 13.5 oz. coconut milk, unsweetened
- 2 tbsps. coconut oil

## DIRECTIONS

1. Take a large pot, place it over medium-high heat, add oil and when it melts, add onions and tomatoes, season with salt and black pepper and cook for 5 minutes.
2. Switch heat to medium-low level, cook for 10 minutes until tomatoes have released their liquid, then add chickpeas and stir in garlic, curry powder, garam masala, and cumin until combined.
3. Stir in milk and flour, bring the mixture to boil, then switch heat to medium heat and simmer the curry for 12 minutes until cooked.
4. Taste to adjust seasoning, drizzle with lime juice, and serve.

**Nutritions:** *Calories: 225, Fat: 9.4 g, Carbs: 28.5 g, Protein: 7.3 g*

# 143. CAULIFLOWER STEAK WITH SWEET-PEA PUREE

## INGREDIENTS

**Cauliflower**
- 2 heads cauliflower
- 1 tsp. olive oil
- ¼ tsp. Paprika
- 1 tsp. Coriander
- ¼ tsp. Black pepper

**Sweet-pea puree**
- 10 oz. frozen green peas
- 1 onion, chopped
- 2 tbsps. fresh parsley
- ¼ c. unsweetened soy milk

## DIRECTIONS

1. Preheat oven to 425F.
2. Remove bottom core of cauliflower. Stand it on its base, starting in the middle, slice in half. Then slice steaks about ¾ inches thick.
3. Using a baking pan, set in the steaks.
4. Using olive oil, coat the front and back of the steaks.
5. Sprinkle with coriander, paprika, and pepper.
6. Bake for 30 minutes, flipping once.
7. Meanwhile, steam the chopped onion and peas until soft.
8. Place these vegetables in a blender with milk and parsley and blend until smooth.

**Nutritions:** *Calories 234, Fat 3.8g, Carbs 40.3g, Protein 14.5g*

# 144. SWEET POTATO AND WHITE BEAN SKILLET

## INGREDIENTS

- 1 bunch kale, chopped
- 2 sweet potatoes, peeled, cubed
- 12 oz. cannellini beans
- 1 peeled onion, diced
- 1/8 tsp. red pepper flakes
- 1 tsp. salt
- 1 tsp. cumin
- ½ tsp. ground black pepper
- 1 tsp. curry powder
- 1 ½ tbsps. coconut oil
- 6 oz. coconut milk, unsweetened

## DIRECTIONS

1. Take a large skillet pan, place it over medium heat, add ½ tablespoon oil and when it melts, add onion and cook for 5 minutes.
2. Then stir in sweet potatoes, stir well, cook for 5 minutes, then season with all the spices, cook for 1 minute and remove the pan from heat.
3. Take another pan, add remaining oil in it, place it over medium heat and when oil melts, add kale, season with some salt and black pepper, stir well, pour in the milk and cook for 15 minutes until tender.
4. Then add beans, beans, and red pepper, stir until mixed and cook for 5 minutes until hot.
5. Serve straight away.

**Nutritions:** *Calories: 263, Fat: 4 g, Carbs: 44 g, Protein: 13 g*

# 145. VEGGIE KABOBS

## INGREDIENTS

- 8 oz. button mushrooms, halved
- 2 lbs. summer squash, peeled, 1-inch cubed
- 12 oz. small broccoli florets
- 2 c. grape tomatoes
- 1 tsp. salt
- ½ tsp. smoked paprika
- 1 tsp. ground cumin
- 6 tbsps. olive oil
- 1/2 tsp. ground coriander
- 1 lime, juiced

## DIRECTIONS

1. Toss broccoli florets with 1 tablespoon oil, toss tomatoes and squash pieces with 2 tablespoons oil, then toss mushrooms with 1 tablespoon oil and thread these vegetables onto skewers.
2. Grill mushrooms and broccoli for 7 to 10 minutes, squash and tomatoes and 8 minutes, and when done, transfer the skewers to a plate and drizzle with lime juice and remaining oil.
3. Prepared the spice mix and for this, stir together salt, paprika, cumin, and coriander, sprinkle half of the mixture over grilled veggies, cover them with foil for 5 minutes, and then sprinkle with the remaining spice mix.
4. Serve straight away.

**Nutritions:** *Calories: 110, Fat: 9 g, Carbs: 8 g, Protein: 3 g*

# 146. PILAF WITH GARBANZOS AND DRIED APRICOTS

## INGREDIENTS

- 1 c. bulgur
- 6 oz. cooked chickpeas
- ½ c. dried apricot
- 1 white onion, peeled, diced
- ½ tsps. minced garlic
- 2 tsps. curry powder
- ½ tsp. salt
- 1 tbsp. olive oil
- ¼ c. fresh parsley leaves
- 2 c. vegetable broth
- ¾ c. water

## DIRECTIONS

1. Take a saucepan, place it over high heat, pour in water and 1 ½ cup broth, and bring it to a boil.
2. Then stir in bulgur, switch heat to medium-low level and simmer for 15 minutes until most of the liquid has absorbed.
3. Meanwhile, take a skillet pan, place it over medium heat, add oil and when hot, add onion, cook for 10 minutes, then stir in garlic and curry powder and cook for another minute.
4. Then add apricots, beans, and salt, pour in remaining broth and bring the mixture to boiling.
5. Remove pan from heat, fluff the bulgur with a fork, add to the onion-apricot mixture and stir until mixed.
6. Garnish with parsley and serve.

**Nutritions:** *Calories: 222, Fat: 4.5 g, Carbs: 35 g, Protein: 9.5 g*

# 147. SPAGHETTI WITH CHICKPEAS MEATBALLS

## INGREDIENTS

- ½ c. Breadcrumbs
- 1 tsp. Italian Seasoning
- 3 c. Chickpeas, drained & rinsed
- ½ tsp. Salt
- 3 tbsps. Flax Seed, grounded
- 2 tsps. Onion Powder
- 8 tbsps. Water
- ½ tbsp. Garlic Powder
- ¼ c. Nutritional Yeast
- For the pasta:
- 1 lb. Spaghetti
- 25 oz. Pasta Sauce

## DIRECTIONS

1. First, preheat the oven to 325 °F.
2. After that, combine the flax seeds with water in a small bowl and set it aside for 5 minutes.
3. Next, place the chickpeas and salt in the food processor and process them for one minute or until you get a smooth mixture.
4. Now, transfer the chickpea mixture and the flaxseed mixture to a large mixing bowl. Stir well.
5. Once combined, add all the remaining ingredients needed to the bowl.
6. Give everything a good stir and mix well.
7. Then, make balls out of this mixture and arrange them on a parchment paper-lined baking sheet while leaving ample space in between.
8. Bake them for 33 to 35 minutes. Turn them once halfway through.
9. In the meantime, make the spaghetti by following the instructions given on the packet. Cook until al dente.
10. Finally, place the spaghetti on the serving plate and top it with the meatballs and pasta sauce.
11. Serve and enjoy.

**Nutritions:** *Calories: 323, Proteins: 15g, Carbs: 63g, Fat: 4g*

# 148. BLACK BEAN WRAP WITH HUMMUS

## INGREDIENTS

- 1 Poblano Pepper, roasted
- ½ packet Spinach
- 1 Onion, chopped
- 2 Whole Grain Wraps
- ½ can Black Beans
- 1 Bell Pepper, seeded & chopped
- 4 oz. Mushrooms, sliced
- ½ c. Corn
- 8 oz. Red Bell Pepper Hummus, roasted

## DIRECTIONS

1. First, preheat the oven to 450 ˚F.
2. Next, spoon in oil to a heated skillet and stir in the onion.
3. Cook them for 2 to 3 minutes or until softened.
4. After that, stir in the bell pepper and sauté for another 3 minutes.
5. Then, add mushrooms and corn to the skillet. Sauté for 2 minutes.
6. In the meantime, spread the hummus over the wraps.
7. Now, place the sautéed vegetables, spinach, Poblano strips, and beans.
8. Roll them into a burrito and place on a baking sheet with the seam side down.
9. Finally, bake them for 9 to 10 minutes.
10. Serve them warm.

**Nutritions:** *Calories: 293, Proteins: 13.7g, Carbs: 42.8g, Fat: 8.8g*

# CHAPTER 19:
# DESSERTS RECIPES

# 149. AVOCADO HUMMUS

## INGREDIENTS

- 2 Ripe Avocados
- ½ Cup Coconut Cream
- ¼ Cup Sesame Paste
- ½ Lemon Juice
- 1 Tsp. Clove, Pressed
- ½ Tsp Ground Cumin
- ½ Tsp Salt
- ¼ Tsp Ground Black Pepper

## DIRECTIONS

1. Cut the avocado lengthways and remove seed from the fruit.
2. Put all ingredients in a blender or food processor and mix until thoroughly smooth.
3. Add more cream, lemon juice or water if you want to have a looser texture.
4. Adjust seasonings as needed.
5. Serve with naan and enjoy.

**Nutritions:** *Protein: 6% 21 kcal, Fat: 79% 289 kcal, Carbohydrates: 16% 57 kcal*

# 150. PLANT BASED CRISPY FALAFEL

## INGREDIENTS

- 1 tbsp. extra-virgin olive oil
- 1 cup dried chickpeas soaked for 24 hours in the refrigerator
- 1 cup cauliflower, chopped
- ½ cup red onion, chopped
- ½ cup packed fresh parsley
- 2 cloves garlic, quartered
- 1 tsp. sea salt
- ½ tsp. ground black pepper
- ½ tsp. ground cumin
- ¼ tsp. ground cinnamon

## DIRECTIONS

1. Preheat oven to 375° F.
2. In a food processor, mix chickpeas, cauliflower, onion, parsley, garlic, salt, pepper, cumin seeds, cinnamon, and olive oil until mixture is smooth.
3. Take 2 tbsps. of mixture and make the falafel into small patties.
4. Keep falafel on greased baking tray.
5. Bake falafel for about 25 to 30 minutes in preheated oven until golden brown from both sides.
6. Once cooked remove from oven.

**Nutritions:** *Protein: 16% 19 kcal, Fat: 24% 29 kcal, Carbohydrates: 60% 71 kcal*

# 151. WAFFLES WITH ALMOND FLOUR

## INGREDIENTS

- 1 cup almond milk
- 2 tbsps. chia seeds
- 2 tsp lemon juice
- 4 tbsps. coconut oil
- 1/2 cup almond flour
- 2 tbsps. maple syrup
- Cooking spray or cooking oil

## DIRECTIONS

1. Mix coconut milk with lemon juice in a mixing bowl.
2. Leave it for 5-8 minutes on room temperature to turn it into butter milk.
3. Once coconut milk is turned into butter milk, add chai seeds into milk and whisk together.
4. Add other ingredients in milk mixture and mix well.
5. Preheat a waffle iron and spray it with coconut oil spray.
6. Pour 2 tbsp. of waffle mixture into the waffle machine and cook until golden.
7. Top with some berries and serve hot.
8.

**Nutritions:** *Protein: 5% 15 kcal Fat: 71% 199 kcal Carbohydrates: 23% 66 kcal*

# 152. SIMPLE BANANA FRITTERS

## INGREDIENTS

- 4 Bananas
- 3 Tbsps. Maple Syrup
- ¼ Tsp. Cinnamon Powder
- ¼ Tsp. Nutmeg
- 1 Cup Coconut Flour

## DIRECTIONS

1. Preheat oven to 350° F.
2. Mash the bananas in a large mixing bowl along with maple syrup, cinnamon, nutmeg powder and coconut flour.
3. Mix all the ingredients well.
4. Take 2 tbsps. mixture and make small 1-inch-thick fritters from this mixture.
5. Place fritters in greased baking tray.
6. Bake fritters in preheated oven for about 10-15 minutes until golden from both sides.
7. Once done, take them out of the oven.
8. Serve with coconut cream.

**Nutritions:** *Protein: 3% 3 kcal Fat: 28% 30 kcal Carbohydrates: 69% 75 kcal*

# 153. COCONUT AND BLUEBERRIES ICE CREAM

## INGREDIENTS

- 1/4 Cup Coconut Cream
- 1 Tbsp. Maple Syrup
- ¼ Cup Coconut Flour
- 1 Cup Blueberries
- ¼ Cup Blueberries for Topping

## DIRECTIONS

1. Put ingredients into food processor and mix well on high speed.
2. Pour mixture in silicon molds and freeze in freezer for about 2-4 hours.
3. Once balls are set remove from freezer.
4. Top with berries.

**Nutritions:** *Protein: 3% 4 kcal Fat: 40% 60 kcal Carbohydrates: 57% 86 kcal*

# 154. PEACH CROCKPOT PUDDING

## INGREDIENTS

- 2 Cups Sliced Peaches
- 1/4 Cup Maple Syrup
- 1/2 Tsp. Cinnamon Powder
- 2 Cups Coconut Milk For Serving
- ½ Cup Coconut Cream
- 1 Oz. Coconut Flakes

## DIRECTIONS

1. Lightly grease the crockpot and place peaches in the bottom.
2. Add maple syrup, cinnamon powder and milk.
3. Cover and cook on high for 4 hours.
4. Once cooked remove from crockpot.
5. For serving pour coconut cream.
6. Top with coconut flakes.

**Nutritions:** Protein: 3% 11 kcal Fat: 61% 230 kcal Carbohydrates: 36% 133 kcal

# 155. RASPBERRIES & CREAM ICE CREAM

## INGREDIENTS

- 2 Cups Raspberries
- 8 Oz. Coconut Cream
- 2 Tbsps. Coconut Flour
- 1 Tsp Maple Syrup
- 4-8 Raspberries for Filling

## DIRECTIONS

1. Mix all ingredients in food processor and blend until well combined.
2. Spoon mixture into silicone mold and with raspberries and freeze for about 4 hours.
3. Remove balls from freezer and pop them out of the molds.

**Nutritions:** *Protein: 5% 12 kcal Fat: 69% 170 kcal Carbohydrates: 26% 63 kcal*

# 156. HEALTHY CHOCOLATE MOUSSE

## INGREDIENTS

- 1/2 Cup Coconut Milk
- 1 Tsp. Maple Syrup
- 1-3 Tbsps. Cocoa Powder
- Pinch Instant Coffee
- 2 Tbsps. Coconut Cream
- Blackberries for Topping

## DIRECTIONS

1. Heat up coconut milk and maple syrup until it just begins to simmer.
2. Add cocoa and coffee in milk mixture.
3. Add cream to same mixture and whip until relatively stiff peaks form.
4. Transfer to a serving glass.
5. Chill the mousse in freezer for 2-3 hours.
6. Top with some berries and spoon of coconut cream.

**Nutritions:** *Protein: 3% 7 kcal, Fat: 83% 163 kcal, Carbohydrates: 13% 26 kcal*

# 157. FRUITS, PINE NUTS AND MINT SALAD

## INGREDIENTS

- 2 yellow kiwis
- 2 green kiwis
- 2 tangerines
- 2 teaspoons honey
- 2 teaspoons lemon juice
- pine nuts
- sprig of mint
- cinnamon

## DIRECTIONS

1. Wash and clean kiwis. Cut cubes and transfer them into a deep saucer.
2. Peel the tangerine. Divide into slices, then cut. Add tangerines to kiwi.
3. Mix honey, lemon juice and cinnamon in the separate container. Mix well and dress fruit with sauce.
4. Finally, add cedar nuts and mint leaves to the dish to taste.

**Nutritions:** *216 calories, 3g proteins, 2g fats, 45g carbs*

# 158. VEGAN MINI GINGERBREAD LOAVES

## INGREDIENTS

**For Gingerbread**
- 3 cups gluten-free flour
- 2 teaspoons baking powder
- 1 teaspoon baking soda
- 1 1/2 teaspoons cinnamon
- 1 1/2 teaspoons ground ginger
- 1 cup coconut milk, unsweetened
- 1 cup coconut sugar
- ½ cup unsweetened applesauce
- ½ cup pumpkin puree
- 2/3 cup canola oil
- ½ cup molasses
- 1 teaspoon vanilla extract

**For the Ginger Vanilla Glaze**
- 1 1/2 cup powdered sugar
- 3 tablespoon coconut milk
- ½ teaspoon ground ginger
- ½ teaspoon pure vanilla extract

## DIRECTIONS

**For Gingerbread**
1. Preheat oven to 350 °F.
2. Spray small loaf pans with cooking spray or line with parchment paper.
3. Sift together flour, baking powder, soda, cinnamon, salt, and ginger. Mix well.
4. Mix coconut milk, applesauce, pumpkin puree, vanilla, oil, and molasses.
5. Add liquid ingredients to the dry mixture, and stir to combine.
6. Pour batter into the small loaf pans.
7. Bake for 30 minutes until a toothpick inserted into the center of the gingerbread comes out clean.
8. Cool desserts for 10 minutes before removing from pan.

**For Glaze**
9. Mix powdered sugar, coconut milk, vanilla, and ginger in a blender.
10. Drizzle glaze over cooled gingerbread.

**Nutritions:** *Calories: 64, Fat: 1 g, Carbs: 8 g, Protein: 3 g*

# 159. VEGAN CHOCOLATE TURRON

## INGREDIENTS

- ½ lb dark chopped chocolate
- 2 tablespoons melted coconut oil
- 2 ounces unsalted raw hazelnuts

## DIRECTIONS

1. Place dark chocolate in a saucepan. Cook over medium heat, stirring occasionally until chocolate is melted.
2. Remove chocolate from the heat. Add hazelnuts, and combine well.
3. Pour the chocolate-hazelnuts mixture into lined rectangular dish.
4. Cool to room temperature. Chop the turron.
5. If it's too hot in the room, keep turron in the fridge.

**Nutritions:** *Calories 120, Proteins 2g, Fats 10g, Carbs  10g*

# 160. VEGAN CHOCOLATE ORANGE TRUFFLES

## INGREDIENTS

- ½ lb pitted dates
- 2 ounces almond meal
- 2 tablespoons unsweetened cocoa powder
- 2 teaspoons cocoa powder (for rolling the balls)
- 2 tablespoons orange juice
- 1 lemon peel

## DIRECTIONS

1. Place pitted dates, almond meal, cocoa powder, orange juice, and lemon zest in a food processor or a powerful blender. Mix well.
2. Make the mixture into balls using your hands. Make 16 truffles.
3. Roll the candies in cocoa powder to taste.

**Nutritions:** *Calories: 58,  Protein: 1g, Fats 2g, Carbs 11g*

# 161. GLUTEN-FREE CHOCOLATE ORANGE VEGAN CAKE

## INGREDIENTS

**For the Cake**
- 3 tablespoons flax seeds
- 6 tablespoons water
- 4 ounces gluten-free oat flour
- 2 ounces unsweetened cocoa powder
- 4 ounces brown sugar
- 1 teaspoon baking soda
- 1 teaspoon baking powder
- ½ cup agave syrup
- 1 cup orange juice
- 2 tablespoons extra virgin olive oil
- 1 tablespoon orange marmalade

**For Chocolate Frosting**
- 125 ml water
- ½ lb dates
- 2 tablespoons unsweetened cocoa powder
- 4 tablespoons orange juice
- 1 tablespoon orange marmalade

## DIRECTIONS

**For the Cake**
1. Preheat the oven to 355 °F.
2. Place flax seeds and water in a blender. Blend well.
3. Mix chickpea flour, cocoa powder, sugar, oat flour, baking powder, and soda in a bowl.
4. Mix blended flax seeds, agave syrup, orange juice, marmalade, and oil in another bowl.
5. Mix wet and dry ingredients until smooth.
6. Put parchment paper on a bottom of the sheet Pour the mixture into a deep baking dish. Bake for 40 minutes.
7. For the Frosting
8. Mix all the ingredients with a blender until smooth.
9. Spread the mixture over the cooled cake.

**Nutritions:** *Calories 200, Proteins 3g, Fats 4g, Carbs 40g*

# 162. COCONUT SNOWBALLS

## INGREDIENTS

- 3 ounces shredded coconut
- 1-ounce almond flour
- 3 ounces agave syrup

## DIRECTIONS

1. Mix shredded coconut, flour, and syrup in a food processor until well combined.
2. Make 10 balls using your hands.
3. Roll the balls in 1 oz shredded coconut.
4. You can keep these balls in a sealed container in a fridge for one week.

**Nutritions:** *Calories: 88, Fats: 5g, Carbs: 9g, Protein: 1g*

# 163. CHAMPAGNE JELLY WITH FRUITS AND BERRIES

## INGREDIENTS

- 500 ml semi-sweet champagne
- 1/3-ounce agar-agar powder
- 1 medium pear
- 1 medium peach
- 1 medium nectarine
- 2-3 apricots
- 5 ounces seedless grapes
- 5 ounces sweet cherries
- 5 ounces strawberries

## DIRECTIONS

1. Wash fruits and berries well.
2. Peel the fruits and berries. Cut into pieces. Leave the grapes and other small berries for decorating.
3. Pour agar-agar into the champagne in a deep saucepan and place on low heat. Stir until the gelatin dissolves. Remove from heat.
4. Line the jelly containers with plastic wrap.
5. Place the fruits and berries in a container. Pour champagne over fruit.
6. Refrigerate for 5-6 hours. Turn the container over and remove the plastic wrap.

**Nutritions:** *Calories: 134, Fat: 1g, Carbs: 32g, Protein: 2g*

# CHAPTER 20:
# DESSERTS RECIPES PART 2

# 164. ORANGES WITH CINNAMON AND HONEY

## INGREDIENTS

- 10 1/2 ounces orange
- 4 tablespoons honey
- 1 teaspoon cinnamon
- 1-ounce walnuts

## DIRECTIONS

1. Peel the oranges, divide into slices.
2. Place the slices on a baking dish.
3. Chop the nuts.
4. Mix honey with cinnamon and nuts.
5. Sprinkle honey-nut mixture on oranges slices.
6. Preheat the oven to 390 °F. Then place the baking sheet in the oven and bake for 15 minutes.
7. You can eat orange slices cool or warm.

**Nutritions:** *Calories: 179, Fat: 5g, Carbs: 32g, Protein: 2g*

# 165. GREEN BUCKWHEAT COFFEE CAKE

## INGREDIENTS

**For the Cake Base**
- 15 bright dates
- 2 tablespoons cocoa
- 1 cup walnuts (or other to your taste)
- For the Filling
- 1/8 cup green buckwheat
- 1 cup plain milk
- 15 dates
- 3 teaspoons chicory
- 2 teaspoons cocoa
- ½-1 cup milk (additional)

## DIRECTIONS

**For the Base**
1. Soak dates overnight to soften. Remove the pits from the dates and blend them in a food processor.
2. Peel the walnuts, and grind nuts into crumbs.
3. Add cocoa to the nuts.
4. Mix half the dates, nuts and cocoa with a fork until smooth.  Make into balls with wet hands. If the dough is too thin, add cocoa or nuts.
5. Spread the dough on the bottom of a medium middle baking sheet.

**For the Filling**
6. Grind the green buckwheat into flour using a coffee grinder.
7. Place the buckwheat flour in a saucepan. Add a little milk and stir well until no lumps remain.
8. Warm up the mixture and boil until it thickens (for 5-10 minutes).
9. Place the second half of the dates, chicory, cocoa and a little milk in a food processor. Beat into thick, homogeneous cream. Add milk as needed.
10. Place the mixture on top of the base. Freeze cake for 2-3 hours. If the cake is too frozen, let it stand at room temperature for 15-20 minutes.
11. Coat the cake with the melted chocolate or icing.

**Nutritions:** *Calories: 328, Fat: 19g, Carbs: 33g, Protein: 8g*

# 166. SWEET CHOCOLATE HUMMUS

## INGREDIENTS

- 2 tablespoons boiled chickpeas
- 4 full tablespoons cocoa
- 4 tablespoons honey
- 1 tablespoon orange juice
- 5 tablespoons oil, coconut or peanut
- 1/5 teaspoon cinnamon, nutmeg or vanilla (optional)

## DIRECTIONS

1. Boil the chickpeas. After cooking rinse and drain excess liquid.
2. Put chickpeas, honey, cocoa, softened butter and spices in a blender bowl. Pour in 2/3 cups of milk. If necessary, mix by hand, folding from the bottom up.
3. If it is hard for the blender to mix, add a little milk to get a smooth chocolate mixture without grains.
4. If hummus is not sweet enough, add honey or syrup.

**Nutritions:** *Calories: 432, Fat: 29g, Carbs: 25g, Protein: 7g*

# 167. FRUITS AND BERRIES IN ORANGE JUICE SALAD

## INGREDIENTS

- 1 cup strawberries
- 1 cup sweet cherries
- 1/2 cup of blueberries
- 1 red apple
- 1 peach
- 1 kiwi
- 1 cup of orange juice
- 2 tablespoons lemon juice

## DIRECTIONS

1. Wash and halve the cherries. Remove the pits. Put cherries on a deep plate.
2. Then, wash and cut strawberries into quarters. Add strawberries to the cherries.
3. Add washed blueberries.
4. Wash, cut, and peel the apple, peach, and kiwi. Add the pieces to the other ingredients.
5. Mix all fruits and berries. Pour orange juice over fruit mixture.
6. Add two tablespoons of lemon juice. Let the salad soak up the citrus, and then drain the juice. Eat chilled.

**Nutritions:** *Calories: 342, Fat: 1g, Carbs: 52g, Protein: 3g*

# 168. TROPICAL FRUITS SALAD

## INGREDIENTS

- 1 pineapple
- 2 mangoes
- 2 bananas
- 1/2 cup pomegranate seeds
- 2 tablespoons sweet coconut shavings

## DIRECTIONS

1. Wash, peel and cut pineapple, mango and bananas into medium cubes. Put fruits in a deep plate.
2. Add the pomegranate seeds to the dish, mix and let stand for several hours in the refrigerator.
3. Sprinkle with coconut flakes before eating.

**Nutritions:** *Calories: 597, Fat: 6g, Carbs: 102g, Protein: 5g*

# 169. PEANUT PASTE (HALVA)

## INGREDIENTS

- 7 ounces peanuts
- 40 ml sunflower oil
- 1/3 cup sugar
- 70 ml water
- 1/3 cup wheat flour
- 1 teaspoon vanilla sugar

## DIRECTIONS

1. Peel the peanuts. Fry in a clean and dry pan for 3-5 minutes, stirring constantly.
2. Pour the wheat flour into another pan, stirring with a spoon. Fry until creamy.
3. Remove from the heat.
4. Grind the peanuts in food processers as finely as possible.
5. Pour the fried flour in the food processor. Grind for 2 minutes.
6. Place sugar, vanilla sugar and water in a small saucepan. Bring to a boil. Boil the syrup for one minute. Add vegetable oil, mix the ingredients, and remove from heat.
7. Pour the syrup into the peanut mixture. Mix well. The mass thickens quite quickly.
8. Put the mass into the mold. Line the form with parchment paper for easy removal. Leave the halva to cool completely.
9. The paste is ready. Cut into pieces and try!
10. Halva can be from golden to brown, depending on the degree the flour and peanuts are roasted.

**Nutritions:** *Calories: 197, Fat: 13g, Carbs: 11g, Protein: 6g*

# 170. BLACK BEAN ORANGE MOUSSE

## INGREDIENTS

- 4 tbsp. Cashew Milk
- 15 oz. Black beans
- Zest of 1 Orange
- 1.7 oz. Dates, pitted
- 5 tbsp. Cacao Powder, raw
- 2 tbsp. Coconut oil, melted
- 8 tbsp. Brown Rice Syrup

## DIRECTIONS

1. First, place the black beans and dates in the food processor.
2. Process them for 2 to 3 minutes or until finely grated.
3. Next, add all the remaining ingredients to the food processor and process it again.
4. Finally transfer the mixture to the serving bowls and sprinkle it with cacao nibs.

**Nutritions:** *Calories: 486cal, Proteins: 22.4g, Carbohydrates: 82.4g, Fat: 8.4g*

**PREPARATION: 10 MIN**     **COOKING: 25 MIN**     **SERVES: 2**

# 171. CASHEW PUDDING

## INGREDIENTS

- ¼ cup Cocoa Powder, unsweetened
- 1 cup Cashews, raw
- Dash of Sea Salt
- 4 tbsp. Almond Milk, unsweetened
- 2 Medjool Dates
- 1 tbsp. Maple Syrup
- 1 tbsp. Coconut Oil

## DIRECTIONS

1. First, place the cashews in a medium bowl along with hot water. Soak it for one hour.
2. Next, transfer the soaked cashews into a high-speed blender along with the remaining ingredients.
3. Blend for 2 minutes or until you get a smooth and creamy mixture.
4. Now, return the pudding to the bowl and cover it with a plastic wrap.
5. Finally, keep the bowl in the refrigerator for 2 to 3 hours or until set.
6. Serve and enjoy.

**Nutritions:** *Calories: 459cal, Proteins: 13.8g, Carbohydrates: 49.4g, Fat: 28.6g*

# 172. VANILLA MUG CAKE

## INGREDIENTS

- ¼ cup Cashew Milk
- 1 scoop Vanilla Protein Powder
- ¼ tsp. Vanilla Extract
- 1 tsp. Chocolate Chips
- ½ tsp. Baking Powder
- 1 tbsp. Granulated Sweetener of your choice
- 1 tbsp. Coconut Flour

## DIRECTIONS

1. Start by applying baking spray all over a microwave-safe mug.
2. To this, stir in the protein powder, coconut flour, baking powder, and granulated sweetener. Mix well.
3. Now, pour the cashew milk into the flour mixture along with vanilla extract. Tip: At this point, if the combination seems crumbly, add more milk to it until you get a thick batter.
4. Next, cook in the microwave for 1 minute or until the center is set and cooked.
5. Serve and enjoy.

**Nutritions:** *Calories: 170cal, Proteins: 29g, Carbohydrates: 7g, Fat: 6g*

# 173. FRUITS AND SPROUTS BUCKWHEAT SALAD

## INGREDIENTS

- 1 banana
- 1 orange
- 1 carrot
- 4 ounces green buckwheat
- 1-ounce raisins
- 1-ounce nuts

## DIRECTIONS

**For Buckwheat**

1. Put green buckwheat in a deep dish and barely cover it with room temperature water. Cover container with the damp paper towel and set aside for a few days.
2. Check the grouts several times a day. Mix and, if necessary, additionally moisten or change the paper.
3. Sprouts usually appear on the third day, but it is better to wait five or six days. Buckwheat sprouts are not acceptable until they have green leaves.
4. After sprouting, rinse well with cold water. Drain, and place sends buckwheat sprouts on a deep plate.

**For Salad**

5. Wash and clean vegetables and fruits.
6. Cut carrots and banana into rounds. Feel free to experiment with their shape. Add them to the seedlings.
7. Clean the orange on a plate to collect the juice. Then press gently and cut into circles. Add orange slices to the other ingredients.
8. Add raisins and your choice of nuts. Dress salad with orange juice.

**Nutritions:** *Calories: 303, Fat: 7g, Carbs: 69g, Protein: 9g*

# CHAPTER 21:
# DRINKS RECIPES

# 174. FRUIT INFUSED WATER

## INGREDIENTS

- 3 strawberries, sliced
- 5 mint leaves
- ½ of orange, sliced
- 2 cups of water

## DIRECTIONS

1. Divide fruits and mint between two glasses, pour in water, stir until just mixed, and then refrigerate for 2 hours.
2. Serve straight away.

**Nutritions:** *Calories: 5.4 Cal, Fat: 0.1 g, Carbs: 1.3 g, Protein: 0.1 g, Fiber: 0.4 g*

# 175. HAZELNUT AND CHOCOLATE MILK

## INGREDIENTS

- 2 tablespoons cocoa powder
- 4 dates, pitted
- 1 cup hazelnuts
- 3 cups of water

## DIRECTIONS

1. Place all the ingredients in the order in a food processor or blender and then pulse for 2 to 3 minutes at high speed until smooth.
2. Pour the smoothie into two glasses and then serve.

**Nutritions:** *Calories: 120 Cal, Fat: 5 g, Carbs: 19 g, Protein: 2 g, Fiber: 1 g*

# 176. BANANA MILK

## INGREDIENTS

- 2 dates
- 2 medium bananas, peeled
- 1 teaspoon vanilla extract, unsweetened
- 1/2 cup ice
- 2 cups of water

## DIRECTIONS

1. Place all the ingredients in the order in a food processor or blender and then pulse for 2 to 3 minutes at high speed until smooth.
2. Pour the smoothie into two glasses and then serve.

**Nutritions:** *Calories: 79 Cal, Fat: 0 g, Carbs: 19.8 g, Protein: 0.8 g, Fiber: 6 g*

# 177. APPLE, CARROT, CELERY AND KALE JUICE

## INGREDIENTS

- 5 curly kale
- 2 green apples, cored, peeled, chopped
- 2 large stalks celery
- 4 large carrots, cored, peeled, chopped

## DIRECTIONS

1. Process all the ingredients in the order in a juicer or blender and then strain it into two glasses.
2. Serve straight away.

**Nutritions:** *Calories: 183 Cal, Fat: 2.5 g, Carbs: 46 g, Protein: 13 g, Fiber: 3 g*

# 178. SWEET AND SOUR JUICE

## INGREDIENTS

- 2 medium apples, cored, peeled, chopped
- 2 large cucumbers, peeled
- 4 cups chopped grapefruit
- 1 cup mint

## DIRECTIONS

1. Process all the ingredients in the order in a juicer or blender and then strain it into two glasses.
2. Serve straight away.

**Nutritions:** *Calories: 90 Cal, Fat: 0 g, Carbs: 23 g, Protein: 0 g, Fiber: 9 g*

# 179. GREEN LEMONADE

## INGREDIENTS

- 10 large stalks of celery, chopped
- 2 medium green apples, cored, peeled, chopped
- 2 medium cucumbers, peeled, chopped
- 2 inches piece of ginger
- 10 stalks of kale, chopped
- 2 cups parsley

## DIRECTIONS

1. Process all the ingredients in the order in a juicer or blender and then strain it into two glasses.
2. Serve straight away.

**Nutritions:** *Calories: 102.3 Cal, Fat: 1.1 g, Carbs: 26.2 g, Protein: 4.7 g, Fiber: 8.5 g*

# 180. PINEAPPLE AND SPINACH JUICE

## INGREDIENTS

- 2 medium red apples, cored, peeled, chopped
- 3 cups spinach
- ½ of a medium pineapple, peeled
- 2 lemons, peeled

## DIRECTIONS

1. Process all the ingredients in the order in a juicer or blender and then strain it into two glasses.
2. Serve straight away.

**Nutritions:** *Calories: 131 Cal, Fat: 0.5 g, Carbs: 34.5 g, Protein: 1.7 g, Fiber: 5 g*

# 181. STRAWBERRY, BLUEBERRY AND BANANA SMOOTHIE

## INGREDIENTS

- 1 tablespoon hulled hemp seeds
- ½ cup of frozen strawberries
- 1 small frozen banana
- ½ cup frozen blueberries
- 2 tablespoons cashew butter
- ¾ cup cashew milk, unsweetened

## DIRECTIONS

1. Place all the ingredients in the order in a food processor or blender and then pulse for 2 to 3 minutes at high speed until smooth.
2. Pour the smoothie into two glasses and then serve.

**Nutritions:** *Calories: 334 Cal, Fat: 17 g, Carbs: 46 g, Protein: 7 g, Fiber: 7 g*

# 182. MANGO, PINEAPPLE AND BANANA SMOOTHIE

## INGREDIENTS

- 2 cups pineapple chunks
- 2 frozen bananas
- 2 medium mangoes, destoned, cut into chunks
- 1 cup almond milk, unsweetened
- Chia seeds as needed for garnishing

## DIRECTIONS

1. Place all the ingredients in the order in a food processor or blender and then pulse for 2 to 3 minutes at high speed until smooth.
2. Pour the smoothie into two glasses and then serve.

**Nutritions:** *Calories: 287 Cal, Fat: 1.2 g, Carbs: 73.3 g, Protein: 3.5 g, Fiber: 8 g*

# 183. BLUEBERRY AND BANANA SMOOTHIE

## INGREDIENTS

- 2 frozen bananas
- 2 cups frozen blueberries
- 2 cups almond milk, unsweetened
- 1/2 teaspoon or so cinnamon
- dash of vanilla extract

## DIRECTIONS

1. Place all the ingredients in the order in a food processor or blender and then pulse for 2 to 3 minutes at high speed until smooth.
2. Pour the smoothie into two glasses and then serve.

**Nutritions:** *Calories: 244 Cal, Fat: 3.8 g, Carbs: 51.5 g, Protein: 4 g, Fiber: 7.3 g*

# 184. CHARD, LETTUCE AND GINGER SMOOTHIE

## INGREDIENTS

- 10 Chard leaves, chopped
- 1-inch piece of ginger, chopped
- 10 lettuce leaves, chopped
- ½ teaspoon black salt
- 2 pears, chopped
- 2 teaspoons coconut sugar
- ¼ teaspoon ground black pepper
- ¼ teaspoon salt
- 2 tablespoons lemon juice
- 2 cups of water

## DIRECTIONS

1. Place all the ingredients in the order in a food processor or blender and then pulse for 2 to 3 minutes at high speed until smooth.
2. Pour the smoothie into two glasses and then serve.

**Nutritions:** *Calories: 514 Cal, Fat: 0 g, Carbs: 15 g, Protein: 4 g, Fiber: 4 g*

# 185. RED BEET, PEAR AND APPLE SMOOTHIE

## INGREDIENTS

- 1/2 of medium beet, peeled, chopped
- 1 tablespoon chopped cilantro
- 1 orange, juiced
- 1 medium pear, chopped
- 1 medium apple, cored, chopped
- 1/4 teaspoon ground black pepper
- 1/8 teaspoon rock salt
- 1 teaspoon coconut sugar
- 1/4 teaspoons salt
- 1 cup of water

## DIRECTIONS

1. Place all the ingredients in the order in a food processor or blender and then pulse for 2 to 3 minutes at high speed until smooth.
2. Pour the smoothie into two glasses and then serve.

**Nutritions:** *Calories: 132 Cal, Fat: 0 g, Carbs: 34 g, Protein: 1 g, Fiber: 5 g*

# 186. BERRY AND YOGURT SMOOTHIE

## INGREDIENTS

- 2 small bananas
- 3 cups frozen mixed berries
- 1 ½ cup cashew yogurt
- 1/2 teaspoon vanilla extract, unsweetened
- 1/2 cup almond milk, unsweetened

## DIRECTIONS

1. Place all the ingredients in the order in a food processor or blender and then pulse for 2 to 3 minutes at high speed until smooth.
2. Pour the smoothie into two glasses and then serve.

**Nutritions:** *Calories: 326 Cal, Fat: 6.5 g, Carbs: 65.6 g, Protein: 8 g, Fiber: 8.4 g*

# 187. CHOCOLATE AND CHERRY SMOOTHIE

## INGREDIENTS

- 4 cups frozen cherries
- 2 tablespoons cocoa powder
- 1 scoop of protein powder
- 1 teaspoon maple syrup
- 2 cups almond milk, unsweetened

## DIRECTIONS

1. Place all the ingredients in the order in a food processor or blender and then pulse for 2 to 3 minutes at high speed until smooth.
2. Pour the smoothie into two glasses and then serve.

**Nutritions:** *Calories: 324 Cal, Fat: 5 g, Carbs: 75.1 g, Protein: 7.2 g, Fiber: 11.3 g*

# 188. STRAWBERRY AND CHOCOLATE MILKSHAKE

## INGREDIENTS

- 2 cups frozen strawberries
- 3 tablespoons cocoa powder
- 1 scoop protein powder
- 2 tablespoons maple syrup
- 1 teaspoon vanilla extract, unsweetened
- 2 cups almond milk, unsweetened

## DIRECTIONS

1. Place all the ingredients in the order in a food processor or blender and then pulse for 2 to 3 minutes at high speed until smooth.
2. Pour the smoothie into two glasses and then serve.

**Nutritions:** *Calories: 199 Cal, Fat: 4.1 g, Carbs: 40.5 g, Protein: 3.7 g, Fiber: 5.5 g*

# CHAPTER 22:
# DRINKS RECIPES PART 2

# 189. ZOBO DRINK

## INGREDIENTS

- 2 cups dried hibiscus petals (zobo leaves), rinsed
- Pineapple rind from 1 pineapple
- 1 cup of granulated sugar
- 1 tsp. fresh ginger, grated
- 10 cups of water

## DIRECTIONS

1. Add water, ginger, and sugar into the pot and mix well. Then add zobo leaves and pineapple rind. Cover and cook on High for 10 minutes. Open and discard solids. Chill and serve.

**Nutritions:** *Calories 65; Carbs 7g, Fat 2.6g, Protein 1.14g*

# 190. BASIL LIME GREEN TEA

## INGREDIENTS

- 8 cups of filtered water
- 10 bags of green tea
- ¼ cup of honey
- A pinch of baking soda
- Lime slices to taste
- Lemon slices to taste
- Basil leaves to taste

## DIRECTIONS

1. Add water, honey, and baking soda in the pot and mix. Add the tea bags and cover. Cook on High for 4 minutes. Open and serve with lime slices, lemon slices, and basil leaves.

**Nutritions:** *Calories 32, Carbs 8g, Fat 0g, Protein 0g*

# 191. TURMERIC COCONUT MILK

## INGREDIENTS

- 13.5 oz. coconut milk
- 3 cups of filtered water
- 2 tsps. turmeric powder
- 3 whole cloves
- 2 cinnamon sticks
- ½ tsp. ginger powder
- A pinch of pepper
- 2 tbsp. honey

## DIRECTIONS

1. Place everything except the honey in the pot. Cover and cook on High for 15 minutes. Remove cloves and cinnamon sticks. Add honey, mix and serve.

**Nutritions:** *Calories 42, Carbs 9g, Fat 0g, Protein 0g*

# 192. BERRY LEMONADE TEA

## INGREDIENTS

- 3 tea bags
- 2 cups of natural lemonade
- 1 cup of frozen mixed berries
- 2 cups of water
- 1 lemon, sliced

## DIRECTIONS

1. Put everything in the Instant Pot and cover. Cook on High for 12 minutes. Open, strain, and serve.

**Nutritions:** *Calories 21, Carbs 8g, Fat 0.2g, Protein 0.4g*

# 193. SWEDISH GLÖGG

## INGREDIENTS

- ½ cup of orange juice
- ½ cup of water
- 1 piece of ginger cut into ½ pieces
- 1 whole clove
- 1 opened cardamom pods
- 2 tbsps. orange zest
- 1 cinnamon stick
- 1 whole allspice
- 1 vanilla bean

## DIRECTIONS

1. Add everything in the pot. Cover and cook on High for 15 minutes. Open and serve.

**Nutritions:** *Calories 194, Carbs 41g, Fat 3g, Protein 1.7g*

# 194. BLACKBERRY DRINK

## INGREDIENTS

- 2 cups blackberries
- 2 cups of water
- 1 cup of sugar
- 1 lemon, sliced

## DIRECTIONS

1. Put everything in the pot except for the lemon. Cover and cook on High for 10 minutes. Open and serve with lemon slices.

**Nutritions:** *Calories 223, Carbs 58g, Fat 0.4g, Protein 1.2g*

# 195. SPICED CIDER

## INGREDIENTS

- 3 apples, sliced
- 1 orange, sliced
- ¼ tsp. nutmeg
- ½ cup fresh cranberries
- 2 cinnamon sticks
- 3 cups of water
- 3 tbsps. cassava syrup

## DIRECTIONS

1. Put everything in the pot and cover. Cook on High for 10 minutes. Open, strain, and serve.

**Nutritions:** *Calories 162, Carbs 41g, Fat 0.6g, Protein 1.3g*

# 196. BERRY KOMBUCHA

## INGREDIENTS

- 4 cups sparkling water
- 1 cup of frozen mixed berries
- 4 cups kombucha

## DIRECTIONS

1. Put everything in the pot and cover. Cook on High for 8 minutes. Open and serve.

**Nutritions:** *Calories 31, Carbs 7g, Fat 0.1g, Protein 0.2g*

# 197. GINGER LEMON TEA

## INGREDIENTS

- 3 cups of water
- 1 (1-inch) piece fresh ginger, peeled
- 1 cup fresh lemon juice
- 1 tsp. ginger powder
- 1 tbsp. fenugreek seeds

## DIRECTIONS

1. Put everything in the pot and cover. Cook on High for 15 minutes. Open, strain, and serve.

**Nutritions:** *Calories 27, Carbs 3.5g, Fat 0.7g, Protein 1.2g*

# 198. SPICED GINGER CIDER

## INGREDIENTS

- 2 small apples, peeled
- 12 cups apple cider
- 2 whole allspice
- 2 tsps. fresh ginger
- 4 tsps. orange zest
- 2 tsps. cinnamon powder
- 4 whole cloves
- ½ tsp. ground nutmeg

## DIRECTIONS

1. Put everything in the pot. Cover and cook on High for 13 minutes. Open, strain, and serve.

**Nutritions:** *Calories 14,; Carbs 35.2g, Fat 0.6g, Protein 0.4g*

# 199. HOT CHOCOLATE

## INGREDIENTS

- 14 oz milk
- 2 tbsps. cocoa powder
- 3 tbsps. chocolate chips
- 2 tbsps. sweetener of choice

## DIRECTIONS

1. Add everything in the pot. Cover and cook on High for 1 minute. Open, whisk and serve.

**Nutritions:** *Calories 60, Carbs 14g, Fat 3g, Protein 3g*

# 200. SWEET RICE DRINK

## INGREDIENTS

- 32 oz unsweetened rice milk
- 6 tbsps. sugar
- 1 cinnamon stick broken into small chunks
- ¼ tsp vanilla extract
- Cinnamon powder for garnish

## DIRECTIONS

1. Mix everything in the pot. Cover and cook on High for 4 minutes. Open, strain, and serve.

**Nutritions:** *Calories 92, Carbs 21g, Fat 3g, Protein 0g*

# 201. CREAMY EGGNOG

## INGREDIENTS

- 6 eggs
- 2/3 cup sugar
- 2 cups whole milk
- 1 cup heavy cream
- ½ tsp vanilla extract
- ½ tsp nutmeg
- ¼ tsp salt
- Cinnamon powder for garnish

## DIRECTIONS

1. Place a trivet in the pot and pour 5 cups of water. Press Sauté and bring it to a boil. Blend the eggs in a blender. Then add sugar and blend until mixed. Add milk, vanilla, cream, nutmeg, and salt. Blend to mix. Pour this mixture into a Pyrex dish and place it on top of the trivet. Set the Instant Pot on the "Slow Cooker" mode and adjust the time to 90 minutes. Cover with a glass lid. Do not lock the lid. Stir periodically until the eggnog thickens. Cool in the refrigerator and serve.

**Nutritions:** *Calories 253, Carbs 20g, Fat 16g, Protein 6g*

# 202. BROWN RICE HORCHATA

## INGREDIENTS

- 2 whole cinnamon sticks
- ¼ cup of brown rice
- 4 cups of water
- ¼ cup of raw almonds
- ½ cup of sugar

## DIRECTIONS

1. Add the water, rice, almonds, and cinnamon to the Instant Pot. Cover and cook on High for 10 minutes. Open and remove the cinnamon sticks. Add the sugar and mix. Strain and serve.

**Nutritions:** *Calories 145, Carbs 15g, Fat 2g, Protein 4g*

# 203. MASALA CHAI

## INGREDIENTS

- 3 sticks cinnamon
- 1/2 tsp. fennel seeds
- 1/2 cup milk
- 2 tsps. sugar
- 4 cardamom pods
- 4 thin slices of ginger
- 2 teabags
- 1.5 cups water
- 2 whole cloves

## DIRECTIONS

1. Put everything in the pot and cover. Cook on High for 4 minutes. Open, Strain, and serve.

**Nutritions:** *Calories 63; Carbs 11.6g, Fat 1.7g, Protein 2.4g*

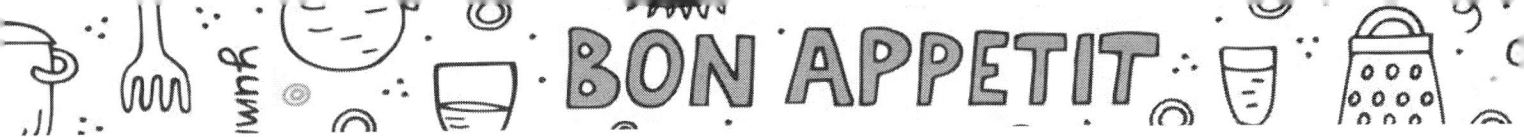

# CONCLUSION

Eating more plant nourishments is related with life span and diminished hazard for most incessant infections, including coronary illness and type 2 diabetes. Plant nourishments, (for example, entire grains, beans, organic products, vegetables, nuts, and seeds) are plentiful in wellbeing advancing supplements and mixes like nutrients, minerals, fiber, and phytochemicals. Yet, plants can likewise be a decent wellspring of protein.

What is Protein? Proteins are found in the cells and tissues of every single living thing. They are chains of amino acids, particles that are associated with an assortment of natural capacities. There are 20 amino acids, nine of which can't be incorporated in the human body and should be obtained through diet. These are known as basic amino acids. Most plant nourishments are considered "fragmented" proteins, because they ordinarily have low degrees of, or are missing, at least one of the fundamental amino acids.

For instance, grains are low in the amino corrosive lysine, however have satisfactory methionine. Vegetables (beans, lentils, chickpeas, peas, and peanuts), then again, contain sufficient lysine, however are low in methionine. In this manner, a dietary example that incorporates both entire grains and vegetables will give an adequate measure of all basic amino acids. In spite of the fact that it was once felt that integral nourishments like these should have been devoured simultaneously, it is currently comprehended that eating an assortment of plant food sources for the duration of the day can give all the amino acids the body needs.

Most Americans get a lot of protein in their diets. "Generally, given the nourishments normally accessible, protein admission is certainly not a significant worry in the U.S., regardless of whether somebody follows a plant-based diet," says Alice H. Lichtenstein, DSc, chief of Tufts' HNRCA Cardiovascular Nutrition Laboratory and official editorial manager of Tufts Health and Nutrition Letter.

**A Plant-Based Diet:** Typical plant-based diets are veggie lover (which incorporates dairy items and eggs alongside plant nourishments) and vegan (which wipes out every single creature item, including nectar), yet a "plant-based" diet can likewise be one that basically boosts plant nourishment consumption and lessens creature proteins.

Not all plant-based dietary examples are similarly helpful. Analysts from Tufts University as of late distributed an examination in The Journal of Nutrition which found that plant-based dietary examples with significant levels of insignificantly handled plant nourishments (like entire grains, beans, nuts/seeds, organic products, and vegetables) were related with lower danger of all-cause mortality, yet plant-based diets with low degrees of these decisions were most certainly not. "The key is to ensure you follow a 'sound' plant-based diet wealthy in negligibly handled nourishments, not one dependent on refined grains and profoundly prepared lousy nourishment," says Lichtenstein.

Research, remembering a recent report by Nielsen and associates for the diary Nutrients, has indicated that dinners dependent on plant protein sources like beans are similarly as filling and fulfilling as suppers containing creature proteins. For a totally plant-based diet, eating a wide assortment of plant nourishments guarantees that fundamental amino corrosive prerequisites are met.

As indicated by a 2018 report by a worldwide data organization, buyer interest for plant-based protein is developing. Fourteen percent of U.S. purchasers reviewed for the report demonstrated normally devouring plant-based protein sources, for example, tofu and veggie burgers, despite the fact that most by far didn't think about themselves vegan or veggie lover. Picking plant-based proteins has a dietary effect past protein quality. "We don't eat a nourishment or gathering of nourishments just to get a solitary supplement (like protein)," says Lichtenstein. "Supplanting creature proteins with plant nourishments like beans, for instance, expands admission of fiber, which is commonly under-expended in the American diet."

Other than potential medical advantages, going meatless only one day seven days can possibly lessen ozone harming substance discharges and add to the general soundness of the planet.

Printed by Amazon Italia Logistica S.r.l.
Torrazza Piemonte (TO), Italy